◆

See it now and live   friend   A rich
thick flood hits the shores of the long pond   and the laid
out fishnet has trapped an animal   Like that
who knows what goes on in a stranger's head?

(171: Poonganuthiraiyār)

from *Kuruntokai*, Vivek Narayanan

mpT
MODERN POETRY IN TRANSLATION
The best of world poetry

No. 1 2025

© Modern Poetry in Translation 2025 and contributors

ISSN (print) 0969-3572
ISSN (online) 2052-3017
ISBN (print) 978-1-910485-41-5

Editor: Janani Ambikapathy
Managing Editor: Sarah Hesketh
Digital Content Editor: Ed Cottrell
Finance Manager: Deborah de Kock
Marketing & Communications Assistant: Chloe Elliott

Design by Oli Bentley, Split
Cover Art by Aisha Farr
Typesetting by Libanus Press
Proofreading by Katy Evans-Bush
60th Anniversary Project Officer: Antony Dunn

Printed and bound in Great Britain by Charlesworth Press, Wakefield
For submissions and subscriptions please visit
www.modernpoetryintranslation.com

Modern Poetry in Translation Limited. A Company Limited by Guarantee
Registered in England and Wales, Number 5881603 UK
Registered Charity Number 1118223

Supported using public funding by
ARTS COUNCIL ENGLAND
LOTTERY FUNDED

Cover description: Against a halftone pattern of blue and red dots is a landscape sketch of a scene resembling a construction site. There is a tall vertical structure in the centre that is smudged with brown. It is surrounded by grid-like scaffolding coloured in blue. At the base of the tower are smaller structures like machinery. Below this is soft shading in cyan blue, suggestive of water.

Above: On the left, the Arts Council England logo curves around in a circle, next to a black outline of a hand crossing fingers. Underneath both images, 'LOTTERY FUNDED' is written. In a line on the right, the text reads, 'Supported using public funding by ARTS COUNCIL ENGLAND'.

MODERN POETRY IN TRANSLATION

presently proximal person:
Focus on Experimental Translations

CONTENTS

Editorial **1**

LING YU **6**
Translated from Chinese by PINYU HWANG

after GAJANAN MADHAV MUKTIBODH **13**
Translated from Hindi by ADITYA BAHL

INNA KRASNOPER **23**
Translated from Russian by INNA KRASNOPER and ELINA ALTER

from KURUNTOKAI (various authors) **29**
Translated from Tamil by VIVEK NARAYANAN

OLIVIER BROSSARD **33**
Translated from French by MARCELLA DURAND

CHUS PATO **38**
Translated from Galician by ERÍN MOURE

ANA CRISTINA CESAR **46**
Translated from Brazilian Portuguese by MÓNICA DE LA TORRE

BALRAJ MANRA **53**
Translated from Urdu by HAIDER SHAHBAZ

LEE SUMYEONG **61**
Translated from Korean by COLIN LEEMARSHALL

IVANO FERMINI **65**
Translated from Italian by IAN SEED

M.P. BONDE **71**
Translated from Mozambican Portuguese by BETH HICKLING-MOORE

LIU LIGAN   76
Translated from Chinese by DONG LI

CLAUDE GAUVREAU   83
Translated from French by CARLOS LARA

after DANTE   86
Translated from Italian by PHILIP TERRY

MIMI HACHIKAI   93
Translated from Japanese by ERIC E. HYETT and SPENCER THURLOW

STÉPHANE BOUQUET   98
Translated from French by MATT REECK

JUAN CARLOS BUSTRIAZO ORTIZ   103
Translated from Spanish by BEN BOLLIG and MARK LEECH

CHIKA SAGAWA   110
Translated from Japanese by SAWAKO NAKAYASU and MEGUMI MORIYAMA

DANA RANGA   116
Translated from German by CHRISTINA HENNEMANN

MOON BO YOUNG   123
Translated from Korean by DABIN JEONG

LEO BOIX   127
Mistranslations of Anglo-Saxon poems

Notes on Contributors   133

mpT
MODERN POETRY IN TRANSLATION
The best of world poetry

'ANYONE WHO WANTS TO CHANGE THE WORLD AND SEE IT CHANGED SHOULD JOIN MPT'

— John Berger

Founded by Ted Hughes and Daniel Weissbort in 1965, *MPT* publishes the best world poetry in the best English translations, alongside reviews and essays that explore what it means to be a citizen of the world.

£29 a year – UK Subscription
£44 – International Subscription
3 print issues a year and full access to thousands of poems

Supported using public funding by
ARTS COUNCIL ENGLAND

To read the best in world poetry and to subscribe:

🐦 @MPTmagazine
f facebook.com/MPT.Magazine/

www.modernpoetryintranslation.com

EDITORIAL

By Janani Ambikapathy, Editor

This year *Modern Poetry in Translation* turns sixty—a year to celebrate a magazine that has championed poetry in translation for over half a century in the face of many existential challenges. MPT is often associated with goodness, a wholesomeness—after all, who could object to the (limited) presence of 'foreign' poetry out the corner of their eye? There are many versions of this endorsement: a magazine like MPT makes the literary culture 'richer' or 'diverse' or 'gives voice/platform to xyz'. But do we exist merely to broaden the literary eco-system? Offer a dose of moral satisfaction? Current pressures can make it feel like a numbers game: the greater the variety of countries, languages and writers from regions in the news suffering their share of atrocities, the better the magazine's moral upstanding. But is this a translation magazine's primary objective, and does it make for a good future legacy?

The answer is not simple: most of us live under governments persecuting their minorities and sponsoring the destruction of other regions of the world. It is certainly of consequence to hear from the silenced, the oppressed, and the ignored, but that's the bare minimum. I worry that translated poetry—from certain parts of the world—stands for an ethically good thing that attracts very

Opposite: In black and white, various photographs of former MPT contributors in three rows of six. Below are the MPT logo and motto, 'The best of world poetry', and a quote from John Berger, saying 'ANYONE WHO WANTS TO CHANGE THE WORLD AND SEE IT CHANGED SHOULD JOIN MPT'. Below that is the ACE logo, as well as a line describing MPT, our social media information, website, and subscription info (£29 a year – UK Subscription, £44 – International Subscription).

little serious critical interest. In the neoliberal fantasy we are forced to inhabit, representation has come to be both the means and the end—racial, sexual, gendered, national and other identities are noted and referenced as if those were the limits of anyone's curiosity or imagination. A far cry from rectitude, this makes for a very impoverished literary culture.

All this is to say that I would like to embark on a fool's errand: to contribute—in some minimal, modest fashion—towards changing the current ethos around translated poetry to reach beyond representation and tokenism. I would like to sharpen our attention, and engage more deeply, seriously, and critically with the poets and the translators we publish. There will be changes to the material—more prose, essays, and reflective pieces; a greater number of pages for each translator/poet; the frequency and length of the magazine will likely undergo a shift, and there might even be some artwork in the inside pages. As we explore new strategies, I hope that our readers will follow us, through missteps and successes, to the shore of other possibilities.

This issue's theme is 'experimental translations': much like my first issue in the summer of 2024, 'Salam to Gaza', a single theme dominates here. The established custom is for every issue to include a 'general' section consisting of poems unrelated to the theme, but this entails publishing fewer poems of each poet/translator—in both the sections—while the overall number of poems appears to be deceptively large. In an effort to pare down the 'anthology' effect, I've excluded the 'general' section and allowed the experiments to run on.

'Experimental' is not an easy word to parse—and much less in relation to translation—but it is productively ambiguous and, for my purposes here, carries with it a sense of the provisional. It is as if the poems are what you read on the page, while other forms of the same poems subsist in the abstract, in minds and dimensions off the page. I've come to be very fond of Elina Alter and Inna Krasnoper's phrase 'presently proximal person' from their untitled poem where every verse begins with the address 'Dear Person'. I imagine that the poems in this issue, are 'presently proximal' (may or may not be persons) and all the while many sense and sonic variants are being conjured by translators in the elsewhere.

In Aditya Bahl's translations after Gajanan Madhav Muktibodh, the poems are excerpted from a long sequence titled 'Mukt' where all that is ordinary, political, and marginal, in the translator's everyday is absorbed by the translation. In Erín Moure's translation of Chus Pato, she juggles different types of spectres between Galician and English—some animate, and others less so—finally settling for an ingenious word not made alive by substance, but by the air that passes between the letters. Mónica de la Torre imagines the Brazilian poet, Ana Cristina Cesar, as an apostrophe made absent by death, who nevertheless turns up in the interstices of her own voice: 'Our voices are beginning to blur'. Vivek Narayanan, who writes after Tamil poems from first few centuries of the Common Era, breaks open ancient syntax with his rhapsodic textual and non-textual commentary. He also leaves us in a bit of a pickle: what is the implication of 'Modern' in 'Modern Poetry in Translation'? (I wonder...). Dabin Jeong who has translated poems from Moon Bo Young's latest book introduces another kind of alternative person(a)s, strictly modern ones—video game characters who threaten to infringe on the reality of the players. There are more speculations, surprises, leaps of syntax, and temporal returnees—more than

I can meaningfully feature within the constraints of an editorial. I hope the poems here will set off many experiments, pursuits and a longing for other linguistic selves.

Janani Ambikapathy

Artist's Note by Aisha Farr: The work on the cover and the ones that appear inside this issue are from an ongoing series of miniatures. I use card and dry materials, paint, and found things like barbs from feathers off the street. For me, their smallness echoes how visual experience feels: mental pictures are flat; small ideas are also material objects.

The image on the cover is from a memory, of a poet, Thiruvalluvar, under-construction. A decade ago, I went to Kanyakumari in Tamil Nadu where two seas and an ocean meet. Looking far out to the sea(s), to the scaffolded Valluvar statue, was like holding a scored but even stone. At sunset, everyone in Kanyakumari rushes to the shore to look into the distance together. That moment—both split and common—appears in the drawing on the cover.

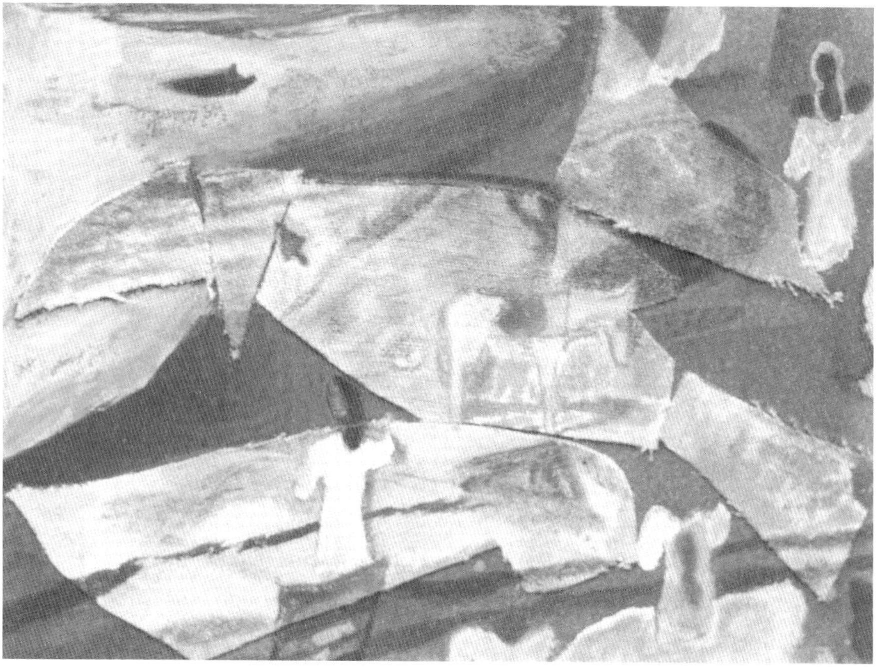

LING YU

Translated from Chinese by Pinyu Hwang

Now a retired professor at National Ilan University in Yilan, Taiwan, Ling Yu (零雨) was born in Taipei in 1952. She has served as editor for poetry magazines *Xianzai Shi* (現在詩, 'Poetry Now') and *Modern Poetry* (現代詩). She is the winner of the 2025 Newman Prize for Chinese Literature.

    Ling Yu's poetry encompasses a wide range of themes, including history, family, place, and nature. Her style possesses a certain simplicity, yet gives rise to a sense of majesty. The poem here, 'Stunt Family' (特技家族), comprises a suite of poems appearing in a collection of the same name, *Stunt Family* (特技家族), 1996. Throughout this set of nine poems, Ling Yu interweaves physical body parts with abstract, metaphorical space and symbols. One characteristic central to the language of the poems making up 'Stunt Family' is the sense of recursion, built up through Ling Yu's deliberate repetition of words, phrases, and images placed in similar but not identical environments. This repetition may take place within the context of a single line, stanza, or poem, as well as across different poems within the suite. And this repetition is spatial—the recursive technique gives rise to a spiralling effect: the poems become a performance of some sort of linguistic acrobatics, faithful to the poems' title. Ling Yu has crafted an orchestration of limbs in motion, of wavering flames, the flapping of wings, rhythmic heartbeats, cycling emotions, and repeated motions, arranging them into a dance of time, perspective, space, and language.

Opposite: Ling Yu

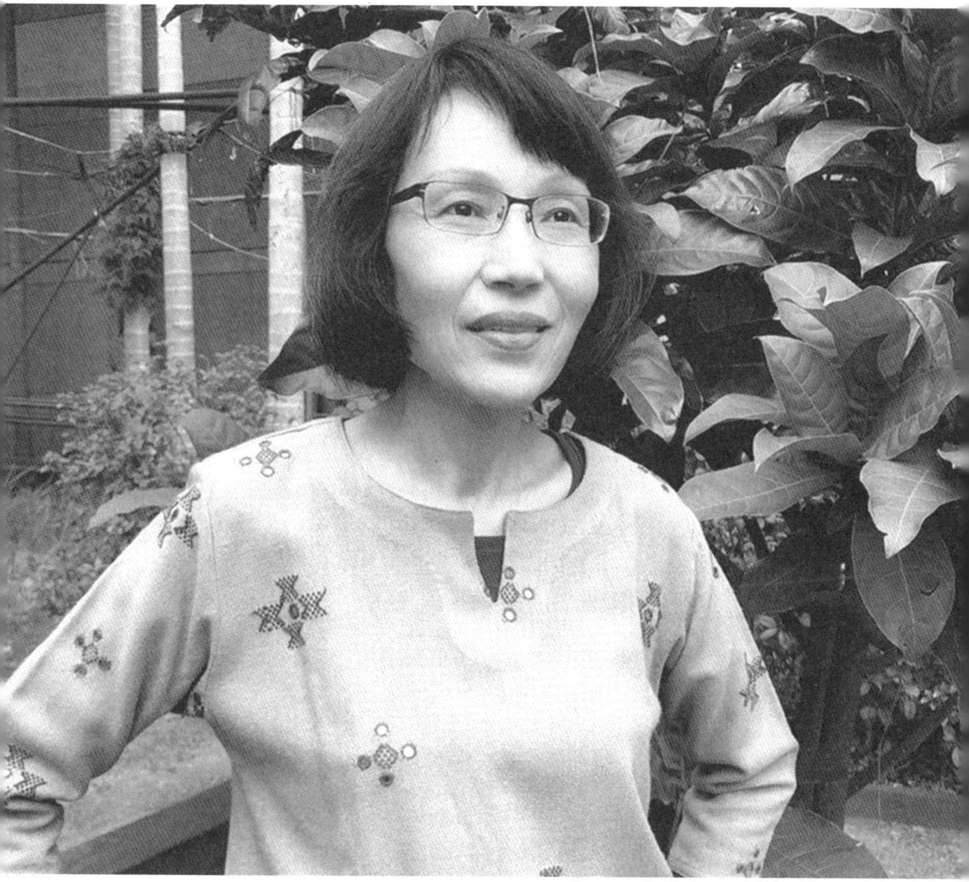

Stunt Family

1 grab two feet with two hands
   jump forward   (to the plaza in the front)
   somersault back   (butt facing the plaza which has the most
                                                         people)
   somersault forward   (in the plaza which has the most people
           shrink smaller and smaller)
   somersault back   (shrink smaller and smaller)
   somersault forward   (shrink smaller)
   jump backward   (and smaller)
   . . . .

   trampled underfoot   (with only the eyes left)
                        (the plaza blocks out the sky with the butt)

2 in a place near to the heart
   prop up a stick
   on the other end of the stick prop up a
   place
   near to the heart

   in a place near to the heart
   there's a small weight because there's a small
   weight so they take flight
   spread their two hands, two feet

   they soar because of a
   stick because a place
   near to the heart

3   the right hand flies high up into the air
    cutting in cutting in   cutting in-
    to the head turns most fragile
    spot

    exploding bricks scatter
    escape then with the sharpest
    body lift off and find
    the right hand

4   soon as the mouth opens, it spits out
    flames. for the darkness on all four sides
    for the darkness has come
    too early for
    provoking you. from within the body
    spontaneously combusts from twisted canals
    scurries out crosses the plaza for

    every person on fire recognizes
    fellow travellers

5   who was it that swept across this plaza?
    with the speed of flight?

    two hands embracing forward
    and void reaches out its hands

    are those ropes that are moving?
    or is it flesh?

(always wearing a smile)
in the designated corner
embrace one another's bodies
and so brush past each other

is it due to speed?
or is it an actual embrace?

land the place of the other
(always wearing a smile)
lock eyes
with each other's void

6   between the head and the arms. fire forms the wings. rotate
the head. arms
balance. find the way
swing between the stairs and
the streets. a hunchbacked person
walks toward the plaza at dusk
swinging. a distant flock of doves
flap their wings and link up their arms

rotate. fire. rotate. all the wings
fly into the air. arms. all arms
lift. the head lifts. convey a
faith of the pure lands. lift. fire. lift
wings. the flock of doves return and sojourn in cages

all the people walk hunchbacked away from the plaza at dusk

7   I know exactly how fate
    has two hands in its palms

       the right hand tosses out sorrow the left hand
       tosses out joy the right hand tosses out
       sorrow the left hand tosses out joy
       sorrow joy sorrow joy
       right hand left hand right hand left hand
       sorrow joy sorrow joy sorrow sorrow joy joy
       right left right left right right left left
       hand hand hand hand hand hand hand hand

       I have no idea how fate
       has two hands in its palms

8   some dozen hands indeed it is some dozen hands reach in
    tug me stab me pound me poke me pinch me

       I retreat to dark corners then retreat to dark
       's corners dark corners dark

       corners examine my flesh. the flesh it
       doesn't have any wounds but for no reason it's sprouted
       wings sprouted wings

       leap out in the applause I leap out leaving
       yesterday's me there I only left
       yesterday's me

       there

9   and so loosened the bindings
      leaving behind a rope rapidly paralyzed

      push open a door and push open a door outside the door's a door
      's world push open a door and push open a door go down
      a narrow stairwell push open a door
      and push open a door. go up a narrow stairwell
      push open a door and push open a door. at the top
      is a door's world—push open a door
      and push open a door gaze at the unreachable land beyond the door
      push open a door
      and push open a door

      feel a length of rope in the dark
      slowly bind around myself

after GAJANAN MADHAV MUKTIBODH

Translated from Hindi by Aditya Bahl

I was first introduced to the work of Gajanan Madhav Muktibodh (1917–1964) ten years ago by fellow members of Radical Notes, a small Marxist collective based in New Delhi. I was instantly struck by Muktibodh's anguished assertion: 'poetry refuses to let my body be'. His poems were long, very long. The letters he sent to his editors were similarly replete with requests to extend his deadlines. Several poems in his *Rachnavali* ('Collected Writings')—a bulky set of eight volumes—are incomplete drafts. But this large oeuvre was not distended by poetry alone. Muktibodh also wrote fiction and was deeply immersed in Cold War geopolitics (his journalism spanned the Suez crisis and the Argentine economy), literary criticism and aesthetic theory (he developed a homespun Freudo-Marxist notion of 'fantasy'), and histories of ancient India (his school textbook was banned by the state government).

At the time, inspired by my comrades' commitment to poetry, I started an experiment. I resolved to translate a shorter poem of Muktibodh—*Ek Aroop Shunya Ke Prati* ('Towards a Formless Void') 120 lines—into a long, very long poem. I began by unravelling the many formal and political knots in the poem. Say, how (or why) does Muktibodh repurpose Sufi traditions of *sarapa* to conjure the capitalist totality? But the experiment quickly sprawled in unexpected directions. Everything that mediated the translation became part of it. Say, several dozen failed academic interviews. Or the diary I maintained while distributing a workers' newspaper with my comrades in Wazirpur. Even the most mundane of experiences—descending every morning from my *barsaati* to buy two eggs in Amar Colony— were recast by the poem's epic conventions. And now, this translation has started consuming even ephemeral handwritten marginalia and other discarded leftovers. This poem is refusing to let my body be.

Overleaf: Gajanan Madhav Muktibodh, photo © Aditya Bahl

फासीवादी आहटों को पहचानती मुक्तिबोध की कविता
अंधेरे में के पचास साल

...सब
हैं चुप और सारीजुबानें निर्बल
हैं 2016 चीत्कार, निर्वल चुप
अन्तरयाल से यह सब गय
मात्र विद्रोहिन्ही।

चढ़ गया ऊपर वहीं कोई निर्दयी,
जहाँ आग लग गई, जहाँ गोली चल गई।
अत्याचार भुवनों के बिछरों में छिप गये
समाचार पत्रों के पन्नों के मुख शेष
गड़े जाते संवाद,
गड़ जाती सभी झा,
गढ़ी जाती गोली...जन-उर-१
औोर्बर वर...
विचार के........उद्भास
बेह......हाँ......हाँ...पुत भर्मी
दहरी आग...हाँ....हाँ गोली चल
...अब आम्रव्याप्त के शोर खत्म
रहान ले होंगे...
गोडने होंगे हो मठ और गढ़ सब्ज
रच्चना होगा दुर्गम पहाड़ों के ऊपर...

मुक्तिबोध

NSUI
2016

WORLD BOOK FAIR

SFI

good morning bandung
(an exercise in deepchandi)

the natives
are winning but

the war has
ruined all the

factories they
cannot rebuild

them the work
ers in cities

are starving
half-starving in

order to
rebuild all the

factories the
peasants must first

start growing
more food they can

do this by
mechanizing

all their farms
only, they cannot

mechanize
the farms the war

has ruined
all the factories

lebensraum

           UNLIKE CATTLE
            HORSES ARE
MORE ~~ASS~~ HISTORICAL, ~~ELSEWHERE~~
   ~~ANYWAY~~, COMRADE WHEN
CHEWING THEY PULL
       THE GRASS
ROOTS RIGHT OUT OF THE EARTH
    (~~THEY CAN'T GROW BACK~~
    ~~FOR ANOTHER 7 SEASONS~~)
    THAT'S HOW YOU & I
    ENDED UP HERE IN THE BASIN
OF GANGA (~~PERMANENT~~
~~EXILED~~) ~~ALAS~~
    W. OUR DIBBLING STICK
    W. OUR CORRODED HOE
    ~~W. OUR COPY OF THE~~
SOME ~~GEET PRESS~~
  JANA TERAI STUDDED
   W. SOME WETTER ARANYA
THRICE ON A TROT ~~ASS~~
I MISRECOGNIZED EVERY ~~MULE~~ SWOLLEN
    ~~SWOLLEN~~ DANGLING UDDER
AS BUDDHA — MILKING TAUGHT
~~WAS OUR FIRST~~ US GESTUNLOGIK

what is people's literature?

1.

       thought
  labor's only refuge—cups
       of tea
  when i first learned to
  make them every
day—or so I thought for
  give me, nemi babu
    i keep breaking
    roti in a sodden
  room in a college
    in a fort
  i wrote eighteenth century
  (been a fort since)
donated recently by raja
   digvijaya das now
ghosts of peasants
   he killed
haunt these quarters
  what is transition anyway?
  more rote rhymes
  i wrote history is history's chakravyuh
    whole centuries whorled into
      this stair-gapped
    spiral-stilted maze
  all i want to write, nemi babu,
    is an anti-fascist poem
  yet all night all these floors

creak with footsteps of dead
   peasants storming the fort
i wrote there's so much east
   on this subcontinent i wonder
    if by morning they will wander
     into the countless corridors
    carved with lecture
   halls abhimanyu
   calls them super
structure—yet, how, nemi
babu—when the nearest
   capitalist lives in indore

2.

    the cups would
    you know
   daily go cold while i
lolled all day
long on a lowly stone
  stool my feet touched
  my groin my arms
   touched my knees
    blind to appearances
   i could write only epistles
  to please my ears

      JUST A BUNCH OF WITHERED DESI
      BANDITS TILL A PINCH OF PEPPER
      SET THE QUEEN'S EIGHT NOSTRILS
                       AFLARE!

GAJANAN MADHAV MUKTIBODH

      in im
  perfect trochees
    (not in english)

  (a posture some will
   identify at the end
 of this millennium
     or the next
      as yogic)

communique #7

      tell me
the name of
the clinic in calcutta
where sunil jannah
got himself psycho
analyzed
      please reply

     send me
a money order of rupees sixty
to be transmitted
telegraphically to my father
and a book either
a single issue of *chinese literature*
or an abridged edition
of *das kapital*
      please reply

>   forgive me
> i could not pay back
> rupees five to you
> but i promise to pay you
> rupees three at shujalpur
> send me immediately
> rupees forty and no
> less than that
> rupees fifteen from *prateek*
> rupees ten for the unpublished
> but accepted poem
> rupees fifteen from your pocket
> depend on me for repayment
>   please reply

communique #11

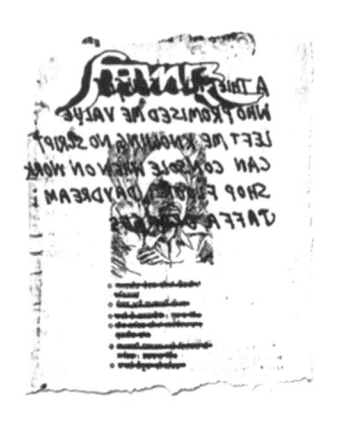

A THIEF NVR CAUGHT
WHO PROMISED ME VALUE
LEFT ME KNOWING NO SCRIPT
CAN CONSOLE WHEN ON WORK
SHOP FLOOR I DAYDREAM
JAFFA ORANGES

INNA KRASNOPER

> Translated from Russian by Elina Alter and Inna Krasnoper

Inna's poems often seem to reflect the absurd conditions of a life lived between languages. The poems recreate a state of partial incomprehension (or linguistic overcrowding), proceeding sound by sound, iterating themselves, each instance of wordplay precipitating the next. This gives the texts a playful but rigorous quality; they're riffs that return, from time to time, to concrete markers of personal meaning, like Moscow's district of Chertanovo or a preference for a specific brand of salt.

But translating with a focus on sound, as well as sense, sets up a precipitous path for translators, who risk total senselessness by relying on false friends—words in the target language that sound similar to the original text but mean something completely different. In translating these poems together, we've tried to be loyal to the original versions but unconstrained by them, keeping combinations of words and relationships between images when possible, and improvising where sense translation matters less than sonic effect. Thus a *сурок* (marmot) transforms into a yak for the sake of rhyme, and Russian neologisms give rise to English ones, like the poor freightened person, both frightened and carrying freight.

Working together has allowed us to keep clarifying and riffing on each other's ideas, inventing new strategies for the poems in their new language. This way, we hope, the intentional impossibilities of the originals—torqued syntax, violent clocks, fish-people and fowl-people—become possible in the translation, too.

*

Dear person,
what grounds are you on here

Dear person, what are you
going here for

Dear presently proximal person,
you've lost your compass
rerouting

Dear person,
empty-handling

Dear person, person dearest,
resting one foot at the rest area

Dear bare-naked person,
bear that away, will you

Dear bale-person,
hardly a person anyway

Dear scope of person
haven't sighted your set since

Dear estranged person,
an honor to show you the door

Dear fish-person,
fowl-person,
pear-person

murston

read backwards   the other way

Dear estranged person's
flipside

Beside you, wereperson dear
sink your teeth in a nutshell

Dear saber-tooth,
zebra, and lynx

Dear yak
and midnight snack

Dear person's doom, the core
of your memory remains intact

Dear pip and pod,
dear puppy

Dear poppy
posterior
per
son

Good person's greatest person,
good name in vain

Dear freightened person
vanishing through the fire exit

Dear person offsite
no shoulder to offer

*

a comet has fallen on my land
rolled off the tongue, unbidden
not again about your tongue, bitte

every night above my land
comets flash by
collecting the tails of my dreams
and yanking them out for good
by the root

every night my land fills out
the district of chertanovo
walking stalking every street the

comet watch
spin-spoke widget
whirlpool pattern

my land stands intact
insinuating the facts
between the let ters

ter-rhetorical blow below the beat
below the belt—bellow

my land billows its train
and glowers crows caterwauls
like a cat-er-pillar

gathers its train
and rolls in wraps up
rushing away from my land the

experimental darkforesters
going by woods by weight

sinking down
donning shame

warn like a scarf wrapped around
fraying out
fluttering forth
for once a quarter
the hour beats the thawed corpus of

the bone-weary station
missing its jawbone

*

good to say good bye to your loved one
so it comes to pass
at every opportune

good to tell your passer-by, I'll see you later!
auf wiedersehen

good to lay on the table all the bits from your purse
mate mote to mote

good to tell your bemated one
there's a stain on your overcoat, a bulb in your eye
strings loose in our closet

good to spot the right salt
and scatter the surplus

good to sleep in
so as not to slop over
not to prop up the ceiling
not to heave your haul
not to hiss or to sing singly
meandering without meaning

FROM KURUNTOKAI (VARIOUS AUTHORS)

Translated from Tamil by Vivek Narayanan

Some Notes on Modernity

1. Naturally I doubted if I should be here. If this was Modern Poetry *In Translation* was I even modern? Was I translation? I consoled myself with a different reading: Modern *Poetry in Translation*. What would it mean to modernize the means and modes of poetry translation? To read the ancients is to be frightened by their closeness.

2. Reason would not in any other way be an elephant's nail.

3. the little prawns / punctuating the water / beyond Arikamedu's walls / at the boatline / where the rain spoke in Roman shards

4. In the variations that follow, the heading of the first page is the title of a poem by Afrizal Malna, translated by Daniel Owen, from *Modern Poetry in Translation*, No.2., 2024: 'Salam to Gaza'. The time and place of the translation both is, and is not, always the time into which the translation is performed.

4. Landscape is there to make emotion. On the plane next to me, a biologist spoke of translating across a membrane. I asked, 'Is something ever gained in translation?' 'Funny you should say that... we do see a broad increase in noise activity at the site.'

5. 'Thirty are the phonemes,' says the *Tolkāppiyam*, in Murugan's translation, '...And the three dotted āytam / Which too partake of a phoneme's nature.'

6. 'Aspects of land and time...' says the *Tolkāppiyam*, although notes that to mix tracts is not unacceptable. All I can touch is the deadness of the wood of my own desk. He said he would come but he forgot. That he forgot I won't forget.

7. On the pendulum swing, writing goes from extension to contraction and back.

8. I see the konrai trees alone, like odd peacocks on the horizon. Human translation outrun, human touch rescinded. So much arid land to cross I thirst just to think of it.

Politics' Corpse Covered with the Morning Paper

முட்டுவேன்கொல்தாக்குவேன்கொலோரேன்யானுமோர்பெற்றிமேலிட்டாஅவொல்லெ
னக்கூவுவேன்கொலமரலசைவளியலைப்பவெயனுயவுநோயறியாதுதுஞ்சுமூர்க்கே
attack?knockmyheadonit?whatifIIdon'tknowonsomealibiIshoutedAAAAAw
hilethewhirlshiftingwindslappedmyfrettinghurtatasleepingunknowingtown?

The time of day is a failure.
Translation is a failure.
The bruise of midnight is a failure.

  Attack? Knock my head on it? What if I
  I don't know on some alibi I
   shouted AAAAAA AA அஃ ஃAA A A A
  அஃwhile the whirl-shifting wind slapped my
  அஃ fretting hurt at a sleeping unknowing town
  அ ஃ A (*Kuruntokai* 28: Avvaiyār) ஆ அHAAA
    AAAAAAAAAAA ஃஆ அ

Destroyed like a salt merchant's wares
in the rain. The rain that marched
like bamboo in his stride.

  Rained-on hill flower-musk in the cool half-light
  Down along the blossom-carpeted heights as
 the flood gives itself to the waterfall he hasn't come friend
  Time of the torrent Evening's big storm
  and the sweet voice of thunder
  He promised protection but then he left
    (*Kuruntokai* 200: Avvaiyār)

Time to scream: AAAAAAAA AAA அஃ அஃ அஃ
AAAAA AAA with
   the certainty of not being heard.
To read authorship. What was the reason
To read Avvaiyār's name. for what
  To read her name.   you said.

30 FROM KURUNTOKAI

The saw-toothed back of the aging chameleon
people going down the road took as an omen
Translation: the fine art of redundancy

Like an ogre's tooth   the wide nail from the huge foot
of a dark elephant bull   head of the herd who'd come   and vanished
like eye spots on rock-drooping sugarcane
a ploughman with a single plough
I moved with great haste and felt the pain

The elephants gone into the desert leave their teeth on the stones
jasmine   Say it clearly May they only break off   sir   our
pure white teeth with which we laughed together
Like the greening fish poured into the poet's begging bowl
stinking to high heaven   liar. liar?
If we can't get what we want   Let our lives also break
(169: Velliveethiyār)   back
If she's afraid she should come to battle   and shoulders joined
and guard   with the help of kinfolk   her own husband's chest
The ravine between my breasts: hating that   he's taken another path
Even in the dead of night we can hear your voice   O sea

Like the single town that forges the public works of seven towns
in its ever-bellowing smithies
Since my head doesn't know any limit   it's my heart that suffers

Old cleared fields now crowded by raucous ploughmen
shallow seed baskets brimming with buds
The time came by itself   Wax has melted from the mould
in the strong bellows of a blacksmith's furnace
                    and the clear split-mouthed bell cast
sounded from rustling groves   But down by the desert path
even as a lush evening feast is readied
no word of the chariot's arrival
(155: Urōdakathu Kantharathanār)

FROM KURUNTOKAI   31

    See it now and live   friend   A rich
thick flood hits the shores of the long pond   and the laid
out fishnet has trapped an animal   Like that
  who knows what goes on in a stranger's head?
    (171: Poonganuthiraiyār)

in a stranger's head, in a stranger's head — who knows

OLIVIER BROSSARD

Translated from French by Marcella Durand

Olivier Brossard is one of the most generous presences in poetry both sides of the Atlantic, translating authors such as Ron Padgett, Frank O'Hara and John Ashbery; editing collections of and writing on American and French poets; inviting French poets to the United States and American poets to France—and here I have to point out how utterly important and necessary Brossard's work in sustaining literary connections, community and relations between the U.S. and France has been and will continue to be as the U.S. now breaks alliances and slams shut doors.

However, us lucky beneficiaries of Brossard's generosity have been waiting a long time for his own poetry—we knew it must be something special, given the intelligence, sensitivity and humor he brings to others' work—and now, *Let* is everything we could have wanted and translating it, at last at last!, is already a dream. *Let* is not an encomium, exactly, but it has the form's sense of a celebration and is a revelation of the experimental lyric/lyrical experiment. The particular section, USOPEN, that I translate here, points toward Ashbery's own early work, *The Tennis Court Oath*, which Brossard introduced and translated in 2015. But in agreeable glimpses only: Brossard's process is intentional, yet obscured and, held in a newly invented form based on tennis scoring (15/30/40/60 characters per line), very much his own—gorgeously mysterious, pointed, clear as constellations rising one after the other. I am so pleased this work exists and to extend it to more readers here.

USOPEN

> I have played so much
> tennis with Age that
> now I am 45; we pledge
> to continue the game.
> Enough to feel strong and powerful
> to keep my game up,
> I fear nothing but Fear
>
> —Charles d'Orléans (Ballade 113)

after *The Tennis Court Oath* by John Ashbery

the face wins here
lovely shadows in a hole the letters
easily visible for one moment justified lilacs
involuntary you arrive easily incomparable real I make myself uneasy I

simply exist here
grass throat and adult skull in cube
fleeing the hundreds of kilometers of chambers
against the bed there is nothing to do without you please it burns easily

I only preserve my
slippery heart in so lovely a letter
that I allow you to lament through the centuries
angry drowned late passes to the tune of a dead world may you make
    your way

you ocean the girl
the person the archives the foam has
morsels the great love lifts we had this country
instantly intangible in twilight the great outside eternally presses

outdoors objects
do not recognize O shadow of anybody
however inside to touch an immeasurable purple
iodine's kiss, I would like to tell you the face's waves like useless saliva

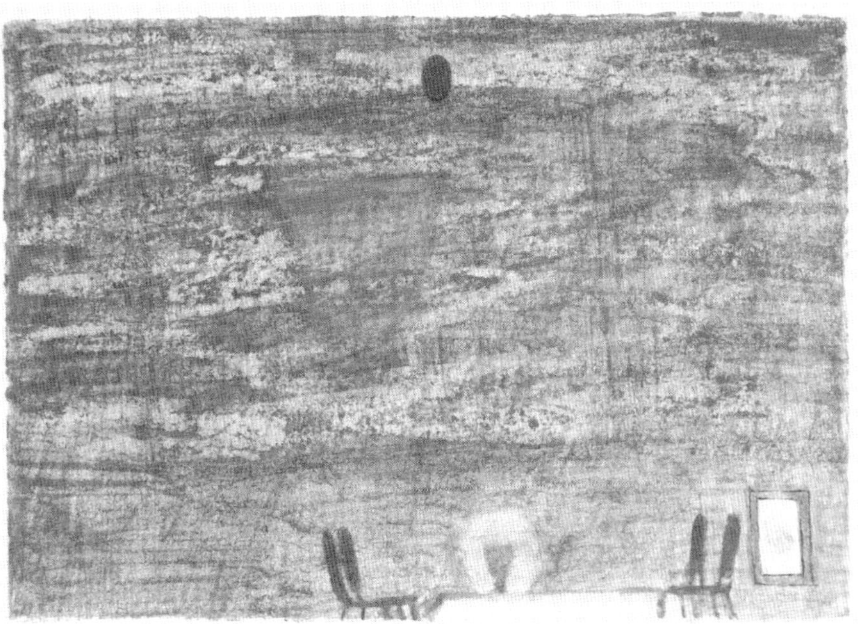

CHUS PATO

Translated by Erín Moure from Galician

For me every moment of a translation is experiment. I'm not just repeating words in another language—I test what combinations of words and rhythms might have the same effect on a new reader as the original poem had on me. In this, I am aware that I am a faulty reader, as I am not a natural reader in that original language. I am outside its culture, though with more access to it than my readers have.

Though this listening and transmisión require a lot of invention, *experimentation* is always in service of an utter fidelity. Given this ethos, I do translate some pretty strange and difficult Works, or don't fear translating them; my approach allows me to listen to them and not repress their difference, allowing them (thus) to affect and change me.

In Galician poet Chus Pato's acclaimed 2023 book *Sonora*, to give one example, there's the word ánima. An ánima has no equivalent in English; it is not (though could be) 'soul', which is *alma* in Galician, and it is and is not 'spirit', which is *espiritú*. Pato uses all three words, and I can't thus collapse them into two words. My solution, which took me a year to find, is to typographically create an echo effect in an English word that is close, to bring it closer to the Galician, and the reader closer to the poem's aura. I added a note to my solution, 'wraith', to explain it.

This is what I mean by experiment. I have to push myself beyond what I am capable of, beyond what language is at first capable of, via a process of listening, of cadencing, of seeing a whole, not just of translating words or lines.

Excerpts from *Sonora*

(15)

In the dawn light she realized she'd fallen asleep in the bin
where kilos upon kilos of salt were kept,
she'd always thought it'd be nice to live on the patio
in the house of salt
The whiteness blinded her
the pink milk of the crystals,
she had translucent skin
white
like birchbark
Did you see her fly?
she ascends the steps of the labyrinth
right to the top
where the planks wobble
where empty cages lie in heaps
where the dust and heat are suffocating
or up to the cone of light shining from the garden
She lives in that house
and in that one
and in the apartment
and in the others

with the wraiths[1]

---

[1]. Spirits or souls of the dead just before or after death, Pato's 'animas' are souls that still animate our world though are not quite in it. *Spirit* has a different word in Galician, though, 'espiritu,' and *soul* is 'alma.' 'Anima' has no English equivalent, and it has a key relation to the 'animate.' I tried *ghost* and *spook* too, but they are too distanced from that essence of fleeing and/or persistent humanity that is in an ánima. *Wraith*, though it does not have the animate expressly in it, has air in it, swirled. Curiously animate!

(84–88)

1
The dream offered this vision
the house lashed by galerna winds
trees bent double

there's a dream-time that operates like a pond, it's there to interrupt
the grasses that shimmer infinitely rolling in the breeze, it holds water
so as to reflect its passage

this pond that dams up and interrupts is solitude
Hypnos reaches out to it
unfurls the twelve wings of the night

who
(remembers) what they see in the waters
the flight of the eagles
that interrupt the shimmer
and prophesy a house lashed by galernas, nearly upended
nearly hurtled across the hilltop ridges and the gale?

a boy learns the flower that buds next to the thorn is a

        chorima whinflower

who
marks it down in the pentagram of the waters and no one remembers
and returns?

the music of the realms returns
the music of animals nameless in Eden
and of grasses nameless in Eden
all the stone's souls

an embryo grows and listens

2
Words were central / at the centre
    words like heart
        store, wine cellar, backroom
        the light that shone down into the basement
        the kitchens, the pantry
        the stairs, corridor, rooms
        Granny Josefa's room
        the dining room, the stairs, the porch
        the summers, meadows and picnic tablecloths
        the basket room, patios, vegetable garden
        the double door that leads to this garden
        the door to shut the storeroom
        the metal door
        the garages, the salt bin
        the trough for pig swill
        and when you finished wandering in the heart
        a heart beat again

ouf, heart!!! tombs

        words of the woodlands or of switchbacked paths
        scented with honeysuckle and trod by roe deer
        and the wraiths

wraith of the father who holds you dear to keep you from death
wraith of the mother / even if egotism is powerful protection then
disentangles you from everything, too
    it's that without loved ones you lose your compass in life

words that are born at dawn
arise to the sky or burrow in the caverns of the Earth
with sun in the West and a view of the waters

every neuron is tensed toward them

3
Because in the misfortune
that was surely that of my childhood
you all bustled back and forth with platters of *bacallau e coliflor* [1]
navigating the uneven floor
between kitchen and pantry
and on Christmas Eve you all hefted those platters
paprika-flecked
and steaming, set them down in the middle

this is why I can't make a mad dash into happiness

not even the neck-wrung bird that displays its breast to the stars
or the premonition that you'll cross the threshold

when you cross it

---

1. Salt cod with cauliflower was a classic Christmas meal in Galicia, like the turkey dinner of Canada and the USA.

(121–122)

We do it with our ears
as the vixen does when she feels the wind

we do it with our eyes
hers are round and yellow and don't shrink from the light

we do it with the image
as when we're transported

> Soul and I
> Soul extends on all sides of the body
> teeters
> at the crown of the bridge's central ogive
> from there we head to the woodlands

we do it with our body
as we do when we measure the height of ferns
and Language says
"they're up to your shoulders"
and there is no landscape
because Soul, I, and Language don't hierarchize
Language sees itself as nature
as spirit
as what utters and is not landscape
is not reductive

we do it with our teeth
as does the vixen with rodents
which she drops upon hearing our footfall
we do it with our voice
as does the blackbird
    possibly
    when we teeter in the crown of the ogive
    we breathe fog and night and the waters
    with the help of the image we plunge into greenery
    and into the wraiths
    restless animal wraiths
    and into every power
Soul's eyes are round flat yellow and don't shrink from the light
mine, slits in a face

    possibly, yes
    —before entering wooded trails and feeling wind
    and ferns and spirit and the wraiths—

    possibly
    before
    "possibly, not having been born"

we grabble

ANA CRISTINA CESAR

Translated from Portuguese by Mónica de la Torre

Dear Ana C.,

The other day, shortly after I turned off the alarm clock, I found myself thinking of that strange short poem of yours, *Invisão* ('Invision'), a neologism that sounds a lot like *invenção* (invention) in Portuguese: 'Ink ran out before the poem began. / Lightness scares me. / I woke up feeling chirpy, feet feet. / Ink ran out before the poem began.' I know you wrote 'before *poetry* began,' but that sounds a little turgid to my ears. A part of me thinks that my change makes the poem's central paradox more tangible, although I wonder if you deliberately chose 'poetry' as a way to speak of the ineffable. Ink ran out, yes, but poetry is elsewhere anyway. Your assembly of four lines perhaps leads up, but never amounts, to poetry with a capital P, you might be saying. No need to bemoan this. It's a good thing, and you're feeling chirpy anyway.

If you were able to entertain my query, what would you advise? I know you were attuned to translation's predicaments from your commentary on the work you produced while getting a master's degree in translation at Essex between 1979 and 1981. Your thesis focused on Katherine Mansfield's story 'Bliss,' but while there you also translated a handful of Emily Dickinson's poems into Portuguese. In your notes, you mention avoiding words that turned ugly and heavy in your versions: *parede* (wall), for instance, in the poem 'The dying need but little, dear...'. You loved Dickinson. Did you have her in mind when writing about translations that, rather than pursuing a didactic mission, result from a passion that blurs the voices of the author and translator? You said you preferred vividness over fidelity, with its off-putting marital connotations.

When I encountered your poems, I was two or three years older than 31, the age at which you decided to end your life. I revisit your work every now and again. Being inevitably older each time I do so, the tragedy of your suicide has gradually come into fuller view. You were so young, Ana C.! Reading you for the first time opened up possibilities that I could metabolise and try to implement in my poems. Your writing's brisk, casual tone; its performative slipperiness; its clever upending of lyric poetry's clichés. I admired too how you reclaimed minor literary genres—the epistolary, the journalistic. I'm no longer the person for whom writing was a way of trying on and playing with different sensibilities. Now I'm trying to hear those voices that I've been carrying within all along so I can wring them out of myself. Perhaps in the end it's all the same, but instead of going from the outside in, I'm working from the inside out.

I've been absorbed in a photobiography of yours, *Inconfissões*, that, in covering different stages of your life, makes you appear somewhat Cindy Shermanesque. In one image you sport a pixie cut and striped t-shirt that make you look like Jean Seberg in *Breathless*; in another, you're a countercultural intellectual in your wire-rimmed glasses. There you are, in bell bottoms and a tuxedo t-shirt, a bona fide tourist in Buenos Aires. I turn the pages and find you at six years old, penning your first published poems. Obedience turned into defiance by the 1970s, as shown in the photo of you in a disco-era jumpsuit facing the camera behind the sunglasses you rarely took off. An early '80s image of you in a low-cut dress and feathered haircut surprises me—you appear demure, feminine, hardly a *poeta marginal*. I wonder if any of this relates to your wanting to research movies about writers for the master's degree you got in your native Rio de Janeiro before going to England. You described your goal as identifying 'what definitions of literature, what types of representations of literary authors are put in circulation by these films.' It's almost as if in your poems you were investigating the flip side of the relationship between cinema and poetry: What types of cinematic representations do the speakers of your poems put in circulation? What female archetypes do their utterances produce? For one, they mark the crystallisation of youth culture as a global phenomenon.

    Last night, I faced the dilemma of hauling myself elsewhere, with a newborn who perhaps wasn't mine, an armoire full of clothes, and a suitcase full of books. Just the idea of getting to the airport with all this baggage paralyzed me. 'Mother, I don't want to leave,' I hear myself say. But the move is impossible to postpone. As I brace myself for it, I wake up. I write down the dream and realize it sounds like one of yours. Our voices are beginning to blur.

    Your silence is sad, but it isn't heavy. I find it welcoming, spacious. You chose to remain forever young, never becoming a Mrs. I hope you don't mind my addressing you intimately now, my accessing, via your poems, a voice from a past self. My refusal of your wishes to be done with it all by carrying your work into the future. I don't expect you to reply. I'm not seeking answers; I just want to find out what my questions are.

Love, Mónica

Clarice 6-4-68

Clarice,
my dear:
you're all one and all of a piece you're all round and all pointy you're cubic and starry, transparent, opaque.

Clarice,
you're a lost case
    (and a found one too)

At times I'll be thinking you're a big-eyed and small-mouthed and sparsely wrinkled middle-aged lady
And I'll feel like going into a white cube of a shop
To buy a mille-feuille, a tad too sweet
Cover it in a wrapper with a thousand question marks
Knock on your door
And hand you the mille-feuille
Being mindful that I can't call you "you"
And that every time I say "you"
I ought to correct myself and say "Mrs."
Though in my thoughts it's "you"
And then I'd go over to
Av. Atlântica and take a stroll on a humid afternoon
And you (sorry) would be eating the mille-feuille sheet by sheet
And after three days
In your *Jornal do Brasil* chronicle
Instead of a mention, barely an exhaustive PS:
"I ate a mille-feuille, I'm foiled and exfoliated."

From *Inéditos y Dispersos* (Scattered and Unpublished)

June 16

I can hear my feminine voice: I'm sick of being a man. Ângela disagrees with her eyes: a woman left lonely. The day comes to an end. Cometh, children, cometh to Jesus. The Bible and a hymnal on my lap. White stockings. The organ dad used to play. Final blessing amen. Tossing and turning on a single bunk bed. Mom came to sniff around and noticed everything. Mom sees into the heart's eyes but I'm sick of being a man. Ângela gives me a hard time with her eyelids painted lilac, or whatever other sinister color from her little eyeshadow case. Cobblestoned breasts. Dysfunctions. Cold feet. I am the way, the truth, life. Your word a lamp for my feet. It lights my path. I can hear the voice. Amen.

February 18

I've gained a lot of practice with bureaucratic writings, letters of recommendation, drafts, and consultations. The unavoidable work of technical writing. At this point only noble diction would console me. But not the dry rhythm of the logbooks they demand from me!

April 19

It was night and a glove of anguish caressed my throat. School compositions whirled about, the ones I had read and had written and the array my mother passed down to me. It was night and a glove of anguish... It was winter and the lone woman... Corners darkened and the wind howled... I set off with joyous school legs, well-composed phrases of pure pornography, girls in petticoats buzzing down the steep staircase. I climbed the slope grimacing, anticipating the cold and the erotic sounds filling the smoky room.

June 16

I decide to write a novel. Characters: The Great Writer with Great Hazel Eyes, a razor-sharp, passionate woman. The ugly fine photographer who sees me at the ready, long pencil in hand, inventing the lost island of pleasure. The little book that slipped behind the shelves in the wall of the room that fit inside the blind labyrinth that the thinking rabbit knew about and knew about and knew about. By then I had a room of my own with a sliding daffodil window and, at night, suffered the warm hunger pangs dad had given to me.

February 21

I no longer want the fury of truth. I walk into an ordinary shoe store. It's raining behind me. Yellow cats circle about in the background. I despise my dear Baudelaire, but I look for a brutal model in the window. Behave yourself, pain; wise as you should be, but not too generous, no.
 Receive the affection locked in my chest. I put shoes on, decisively, where the cats pretend to love me, youthful, real. I used to be a 36, a Cinderella, tiptoeing, little thumb, pay at the cash register, pick up in front. My pain. Hold my hand. Come here, away from the others. Listen, my dear, listen. Tonight's march. Leaning over the years in this pulse. Very nice. I have everything that hurts. The German women marching as if they were men. The best scenes in the novel, the author knew not how to comment on them. Don't leave me now, beast.

Midnight, June 16

I can't return to letters, they hurt like a catastrophe. I no longer write. I no longer militate. I'm in the middle of a scene, between those who adore me and those whom I adore. Here at the center, I feel my flustered face, my frozen hands, a burning in my throat. The London pack hunts my silly naughtiness, a candid seduction that gives and takes and commands respect, madame wild boar. I can't stand perfumes. I sniff his suit. A Mia Farrow air, translucid. The horror of perfumes, of jealousy, of the shoe—that perfect twin of dark jealousy shining bright in my throat. The brides I prepared, beloveds, white. Daughters of night's horror, bursting with newness, slap-happy with their bouquets. So sad when it dies out, sweet, sleepless, my love.

BALRAJ MANRA

Translated from Urdu by Haider Shahbaz

Balraj Manra was an Indian modernist and Marxist writer who changed the course of Urdu literature with a handful of hybrid prose-poetry 'compositions', which were published in small, independent literary journals in the sixties and seventies. In 1964, Manra published his first composition: 'Composition December '64'. It was an abstract presentation of several disconnected images and ideas: descriptions of Delhi's literary coffeehouses, commentary on communist politics, song lyrics, notes on modernity, and overheard conversations. The text did not move from sentence to sentence, right to left (in Urdu), top to bottom. Instead, it was scattered across the page without any consideration for the protocols of continuous prose. From 1964 to 1971, Manra published more compositions. These texts relied on surrealist visions and formal experiments that explored the connections between modernist aesthetics and Marxist politics. Due to their inventive imagery, structure, and form, Manra's compositions opened a new path in Urdu modernism, at a time when, according to critic, Shamim Hanfi, 'poetry and prose were still strictly distinguished in Urdu literature, and before any strong or stable avant-garde tradition had appeared.' In 1971, Manra published 'The Last Composition.' He never published another composition or any other creative text after 'The Last Composition'. Insead, he dedicated himself to the occasional critical essay and the editing of his literary magazine, *Shaoor* ('Knowledge'), where he published the work of avant-garde Urdu writers like Enver Sajjad and Sara Shagufta, as well as translations of Antonio Gramsci, Bertolt Brecht, Reza Baraheni, and Emmanuil Kazakevich.

Overleaf: Balraj Manra

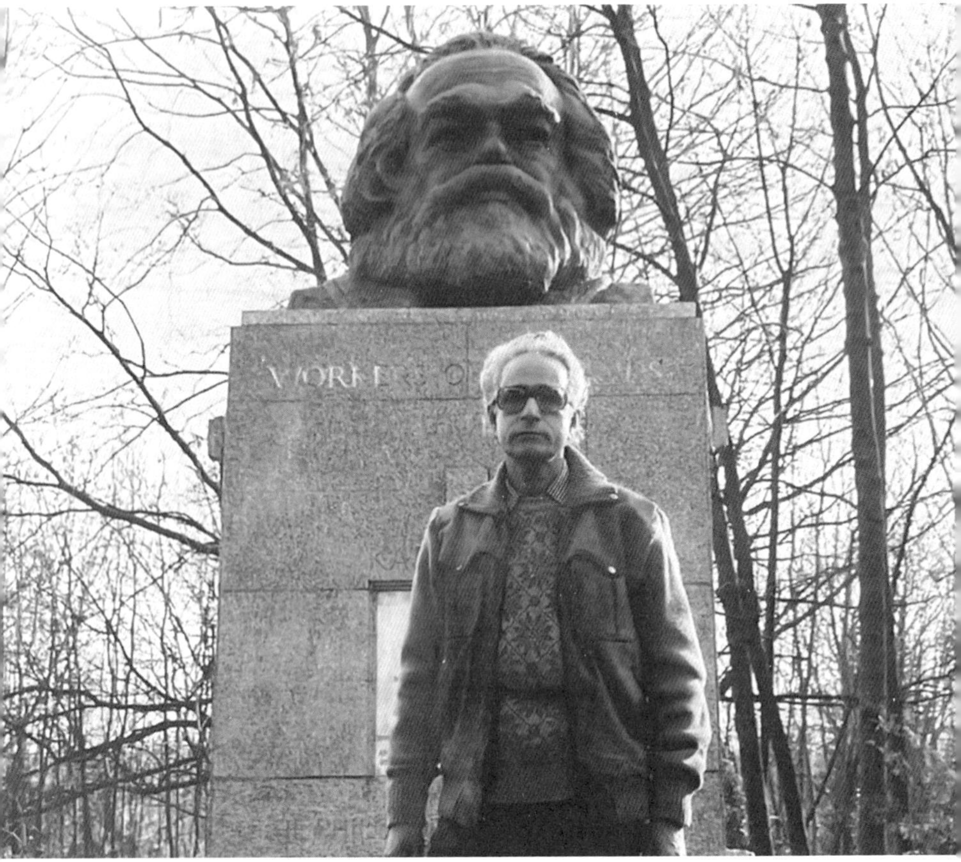

Composition 5

Day dust rises: frightened eyes watch the fall of the city's arrogance.

Gigantic Eiffel Tower particles particles shards shards absent and the city of the city with buildings turned into smoke where cockroaches, cacti, and crucifixes shelter.

Day dust settles: the city's arrogance booted kicked to the threshold.

Night comes: the night is not like the previous nights: the night is not gendered.

Kids carry slingshots made from ribs and veins of the Eiffel Tower, and their pockets are full of parts and particles, and their scorching boiling eyes are expectant – when the hand with pulsating veins is raised, the night trembles.

Slingshots are pulled taut – and when they slackened, scorching boiling eyes were tranquil – innumerable skulls were crushed particles.

Kids kick the skulls lining the city's border high into the air.

Over there, tired tired people, tired tired unconscious, and those who were not unconscious, were not tired tired, they were expectant.

The skulls land on grand mansions: the grand mansions dissolve into thin air.

And those who were not unconscious, were not tired tired, they were expectant – they tore apart the city's slicing cutting enclosures – that day, that scorching hot day –

Innumerable scorching hot days:

Whether a day is hot or cold or wet, it is a wave:

A wave that comes and passes:

A wave in time's sea, at times, calm, at times, furious: what could it mean? (!)

The afternoon of that hot scorching day, dust flying, trees twisted twisted, I heard: They have adorned their brown hair with currency notes of five thousand each.

BALRAJ MANRA

The evening hiccupped constantly so I met the old man red exiled European in the restaurant where the back door opens to the trail of the departed.

Someone knocked on my door that deep dark curfewed night.

I opened the door.

He lay on the stairs.

I fixed the circle of light flowing from my torch on him and saw that he was dead.

Engraved on the forehead of the corpse: Gautam Nilambar.

I returned to my room, opened the window, pulled out my chair, sat down, looked outside: rusted sky, unhealing night.

As soon as I heard the morning's first footsteps, I saw that Gautam Nilambar's cold flesh was turning into soil. The footsteps quickened: cold flesh and bones turning into soil. The first ray of light: corpse turning into soil.

I laughed wildly.

Then there was no one there – and that's what I wanted – and that's what he wanted that no one should be there, no one should be anywhere, and where he came from, there was no one there, but there, he spent so many days wandering and loitering that he would run into himself in the wilderness of streets and markets, and there were explosions, powerful shattering explosions, and he thought, if I keep running into myself, the oblivious city will wake up from its slumber, he wanted to feel the pleasure of colliding with himself until he shattered into particles but he could not accept the cost: the oblivious city waking up from its slumber – he left the city and mountain mountain he carried the fear, maybe someone like him is there, here, he arrived there, here.

The sequence of mountains stopped under his feet: below, the sea, and to the right, the river irrigated the mountain gentle as it merged into the sea calm, and to the left, a series of stairs on the mountain's slope and a silent jungle, more green more evergreen than any jungle: the sky, blue, and the folds of the trail, summer-clear.

The folds were meaningless. He did not wish to return.

The river itself was merging into the sea, the jungle could not extend into the sea, and the mountain movement had stopped suddenly like it was scared to drown – and sea?

Innumerable suns rose from the sea, innumerable suns drowned in the sea, and innumerable suns drowned in his eyes: he fought arms and legs, limb limb, crashing into waves.

Far away, the shore.

The shore was the beginning of the desert: there was no one there.

: there are two suns, one is in the sky, and the other is scattered particle particle in the desert.

Sand under the feet, sand over the head, sand in the eyes, sand in the mouth: he cleaned himself with clear sparkling water from the stream.

Now he dreams in front of me singular absent singular present.

We are standing against the railing, two hours have passed, we coincidentally came face to face, we stopped walking, we hugged, I am smoking my eighth cigarette, and I have been silent for two hours as he has been silent for two hours. I want to ask him many questions and I don't know if he wants to ask me many questions or not.

He glances at me, smiles, and I know. He says: "Come, my friend, let's get coffee – black coffee, piping hot and pungent."

We are sitting right where we spent ten years of our life, and I cannot say with any confidence if they were ten significant years or ten insignificant years, we are drinking coffee, we are silent. I am smoking my ninth cigarette. One cigarette remains and I will smoke smoke finish that one soon too and then I will leave to get more cigarettes and when I return, he will not be there, yes, when I lift the cup, there will be a note underneath "another time":

But when, where?

The city of the coming tomorrow: dense celeste tear gas.

The city of the coming tomorrow, innumerable recognizable and understandable voices, where "MY NAME YOUR NAME VIETNAM VIETNAM" is the weapon of revolt revolution rebellion riot from east to west, north to south, morning and night.

Who is he? He is an exiled red citizen.

Who am I? I am he.

And he (my) chair?!

Long, incredibly long legs. Long, incredibly long arms. Tall, incredibly tall back: the chair faces west.

The long, incredibly long arms resting on the long, incredibly long arms of the chair: fallen palms, fallen fingers. Long, dangling legs stretched towards the earth. Empty mind. Absent heartbeat. Still, lifeless body.

And those eyes – breathing eyes, bright eyes – big eyes – lifeless body and breathing eyes, breathing eyes and lifeless body – who is whose breath and who is whose death?

The still, lifeless body on the chair facing west,

The breathing, bright eyes imprisoned in the still and lifeless body,

In front of the eyes, mirror (book?!),

Mirror?!

A wall of mirror stretching all the way north!

A wall of mirror stretching all the way south!!

A wall of mirror stretching all the way to the sky!!!

In front of the eyes, mirror,

Clean, clear, sterile:

I lit my cigarette.

He is a red citizen and I am him. There is some confusion? I am him and he is a red citizen. Why am I not the red citizen? Me...I am the red citizen...no, no, I am not the red citizen. This is the problem of my text's 'I'...and my text...Me and my text's 'I'...

...an endless war...

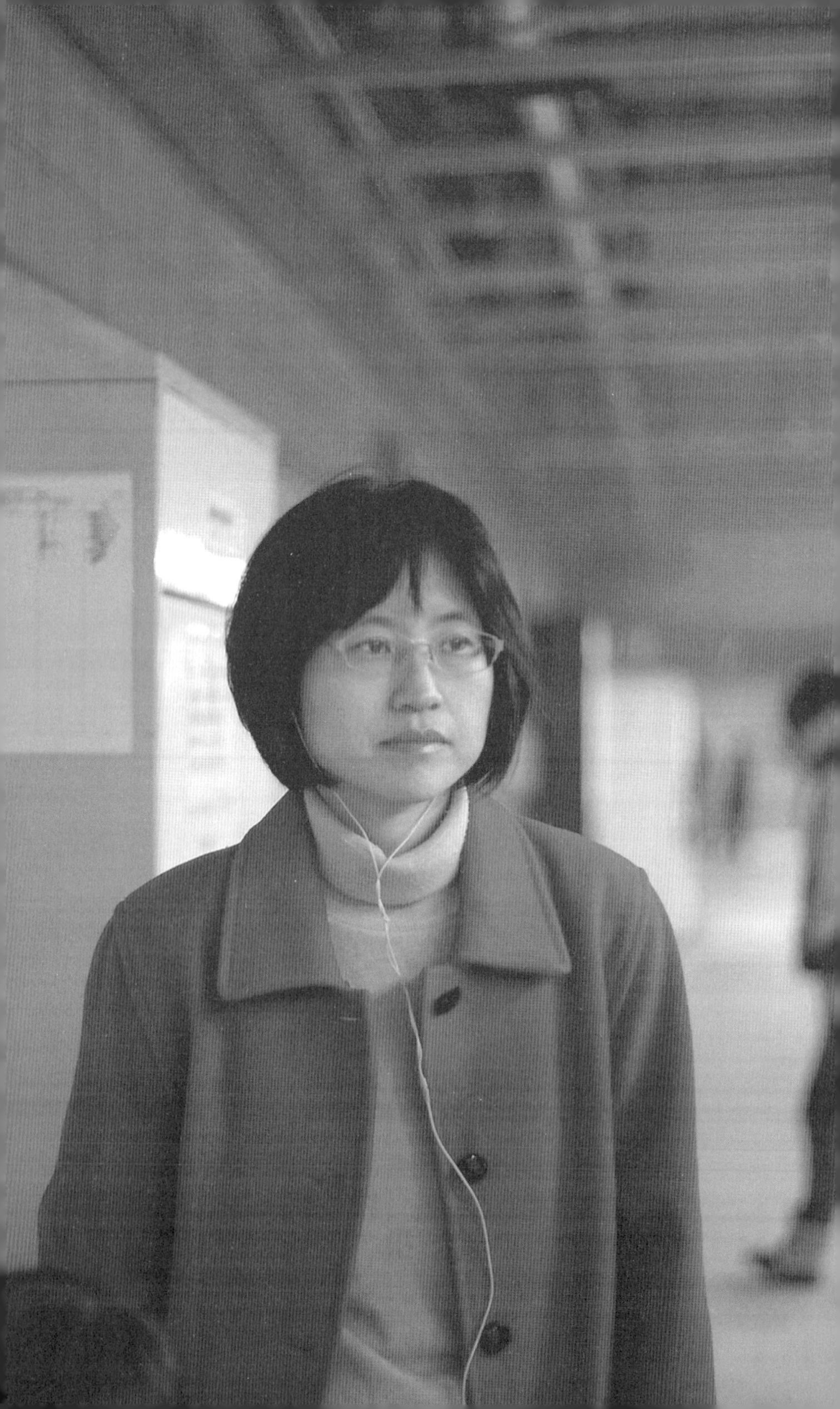

LEE SUMYEONG

Translated from Korean by Colin Leemarshall

Lee Sumyeong's poetry is deceptively fissiparous. As her poems unfold, their apparently simple objects fracture and refract across the complexly equivocal lines. Take, for instance, the poem 'in the case of spiders moving'. So kinetic are its objects—the spiders, the green, the walls—that the predicative relationships seem constantly to shift and rearrange themselves. Confronted with this play of endophoric transpositions and sylleptic splittings, the reader cannot adequately track the spiders' multifurcated 'course of movement'—nor can the language comprehensively represent this movement.

In teeming with potentialities that are only partially chartable, such fissiparous writing seems already to be proximate to translation. By my lights, a given Lee poem is but one "allopoem" scooped out from the turbulent allopoetic waters that roil invisibly beneath it. The translator who comes into contact with these waters (and with the allopoems pullulating therein) must decide which inflections to indulge and which to elide. My own preference for the slightly off-kilter (as evinced, for example, in the postposed modifier in the title of the above-mentioned poem) would perhaps not be shared by another Lee translator. All I can hope is that my choices not only preserve some of the fissiparous density of Lee's Korean, but that they also hint at a wealth of other potential inflections roiling beneath.

Each of the following translations is taken from Lee's 2011 book *Always So Many Rains*.

Opposite: Lee Sumyeong

palm throwing

Spent them. More days
into more fragments
was gathered.
A day of fracturing light
like this I was full of fractured light
fully
absent

I rashly became it.
Became it and made me.
Became it and blocked me.
Moved the earth in the mouth.
In need of earth

plucked the contours that had descended onto the ground.
Became it and I
broke out of my head.
I occurred through it.
Outside of me

cavorting through limit-exceeding errors.

I grew faint by degrees
and somewhere into the drought of light I was endlessly
throwing my palms.

in the case of spiders moving

In the case of spiders moving
into moving green
they are attempting to keep the green walls alive.
The arrangements of the edgeless walls

in the case of spiders moving
to ruffle diagrams moving from their own bodies
they become the most forcefully contrary green.
Let's arrange the agitated structures.

Let's jump down from the spiders.

Can we not become one with the spiders
without mixing with the spiders

in the case of spiders moving
like the inclusion of their course of movement
like their staying always within a larger clump of spiders
they are thrown from spider to spider.

Thoughts once again receding into spiders

a certain sleeve

A memory that kept hanging from a certain sleeve

well the interior of the house was completely empty. A delivered box I love you the bread cut only after being eaten

the lost ear was as heavy as stone as it floated along.

I had to turn in the stair on which I stood because it was too flat.

Certain patterns discard memories then begin. The memories are not well made. The scream appeared only after the pattern of the scream was left to flow into the far distance.

The squares pouring out when the box was dropped, if you walk into the squares a feather will descend from somewhere in this world and

I miss the firm arm

sleeves newly birthed whenever the bridge pillars are rotated
when pulling on the sleeves
from someone's long sleeves
where the sleeves had staggered and collapsed

a memory that kept hanging

IVANO FERMINI

Translated from Italian by Ian Seed

It was in 2010, when I was researching for my PhD in Italian literature, that I first came across a handful of poems by Ivano Fermini in a little-known anthology.[1] I was struck by their fractured, yet compelling and strangely beautiful language. Fermini's voice is unique and immediately recognisable. It was only after some time spent tracking down Milo De Angelis, who was editor, mentor and friend to Fermini, that I discovered he had died in 2004.

Fermini was born in 1948 in San Paolo, a small village near Bolzano in the Alps. Most of his adult life he lived with his sister in a flat in a working-class area of San Siro in Milan, suffering from recurring bouts of mental illness. He published two collections in his lifetime: *Bianco allontanato* (Banished White), 1985, and *Nati incendio* (Fire Births), 1990. Both these collections are now long out of print. In 2022 I translated a selection of his poetry, *The River Which Sleep Has Told Me* (the title taken from the lines of one of his poems), published in a bilingual edition by The Fortnightly Review Odd Volumes. The translations here in MPT are new, part of a project to translate more of his poetry. I hope they will tempt readers into exploring his work further.

It is impossible in English to render the power of Ivano Fermini's original Italian. However, even in translation, these poems, especially when read together as part of a kind of epic whole, yield their own rich combination of imagery and music to readers prepared to have their expectations disrupted line by line, word by word.

---

[1] See *Italian Poetry 1950 to 1990*, translated and edited by Gayle Ridinger, co-edited by Gian Paolo Renello (Boston: Dante University Press, 1996).

from *Banished White*

they were saying gold rain of gold
the colours will not escape
passing through
the little girl's room of poppies and mud

in the dumb clockface
the unmatched skin of the blind man
comes closer to our thoughts

after him the undertow
and with a shiver I pass
through the eye of the needle
the liquids of the tunnelling machine
in my hand

free

from the sky

*

at the far end of the line
is
only
a splinter of glass
and the fish opens its mouth
on the pebbles in a winter place

halfway along the pole it's time and still the moon

returning into its pore
cracks new fingers
full on a thousand years when green

light of leaves arises

*

harmony

each one in the polish of winter
called in this way by the main lighthouse
they bow, wait still in their cloaks
and the confrontation ends with the kiss of bones

in the dim light: they hammer in names

uprooted in the white place
how grateful they find themselves
to be finally strangled
so far as I'm able to give voice

*

afternoon – ball and bone –
the tiniest nut in the
head where the filigree gnashes
lit up
in a man with grass hands: one man a thousand

*

the rotation of a word is nothing but dust
falling forward
perhaps my eyelashes come undone
perhaps the leaves swell larger
without mercy they touch they walk on

from *Fire Births*

houses

the feelings of the pearl
sphere the pale cloth which my mother
travels towards me
it is not after all a hand you don't say that
but black clouds in the wine
the sky and feet
the cotton of sentinels I come to tell you
can't have anything nor dry
perhaps tall stories in the sea
which way which way which way
wash your hair in the gully-holes

shattered line

in the stink you shake your nose
in spite of it being dumb
and bent on staying in the roof-gutter
looking out into immensity
when I see you

a bridge will become an oven
and I pass now for someone who's calm
and the earth
to the strange lemon of things
you always tremble before the big names
those which nobody speaks
but meanwhile I'm afraid that first and first of all
you've muddled everything
the will of the tunnel
ends in flowers
sleep which poetry told I'm going to reunite
and graze among the dead sheets

*

the hoard it's this which counts
how beautiful to her
from numerous canons of leaves
the springs of a lion
all hidden in a drop
falling from my nose
to the wind I haven't given much thought
like a sword which is taller than a doll
a blow
superb sailors
we've just been granted permission to walk around
those things which brief thoughts unchain

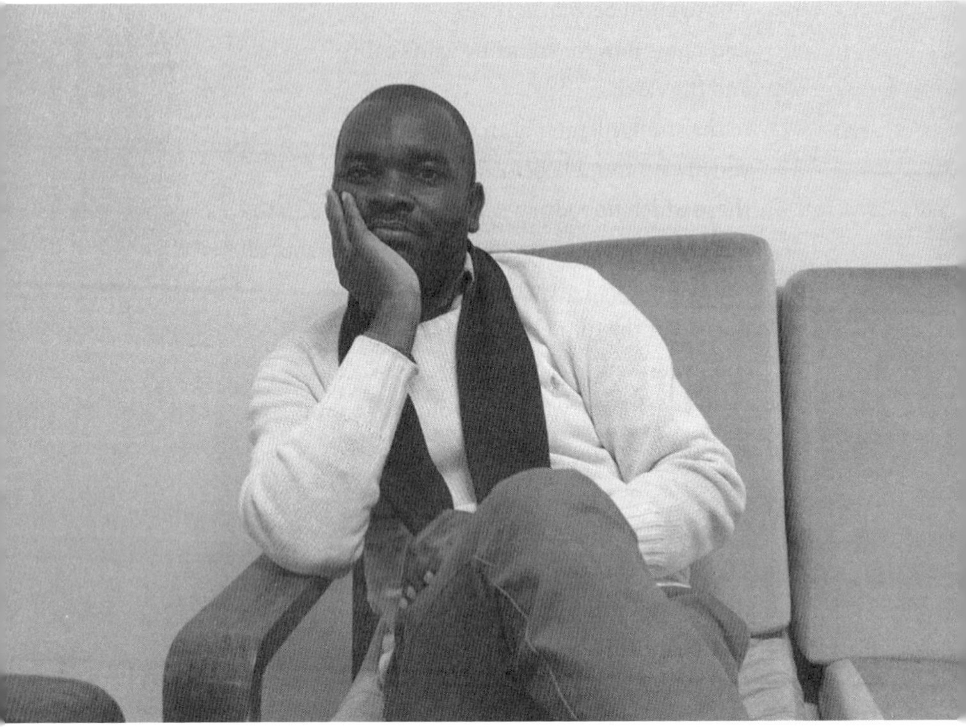

M.P. BONDE

Translated from Mozambican Portuguese by
Beth Hickling-Moore

The following poems are translated from M.P. Bonde's prize-winning prose-poetry collection, *A descrição das sombras* ('Describing Shadows'), a work divided into what the poet calls four 'moments'. Three of these 'moments' reflect on the author's different states of self, the other on his experiences in love.

Bonde's poems are self-contained portals, every one existing in a 'moment' of his collection and time-stamped with the exact date, hour and minute of composition. Each is its own vignette in which time seems to stop almost entirely to allow for reflection on life's minutiae: the way winter sunlight reflects on bedsheets, how droplets of juice trickle down a surface, the way in which clouds shapeshift, the sweetness of tea. The poet asks himself questions, pausing for thought or launching into streams of consciousness and observations on sights, sounds or tastes around him.

The abstract nature of the poems leaves them very much open to interpretation and experimentation in translation. In working with the poems here, I have paid particular attention to sound, sometimes diverging more boldly from the original Portuguese to reflect the sonorous, often dream-like qualities of Bonde's words. For example, *barco* ('boat') becomes 'dhow-boat': a looser translation but one that mirrors the Portuguese sounds and syllables as well as nodding to a vessel that is inherently Mozambican. Similarly, *onde brincas* ('where you play') becomes 'on the brink of playing', thus experimenting with and retaining the sounds from the source while exploring shades of meaning. The line, '*rio um par de nuvens*' ('I laugh/River a pair of clouds'), its double meaning ripe for experimentation, becomes 'I bellow a river of cloud-couplets', simultaneously retaining the psychedelic qualities of the original and taking on its own new form of bizarreness.

Opposite: MP Bonde

Desire

I want to be the portal, the open field on the brink of playing silences. It: can-open-air our quenched afternoons colluding. Mystery emerging in corporeal solitude. I want to be magic kidnapped kisses: dusk's latening voluptuousness unfurls the mango branches. What walking lightness, raven-black, translucent, (...) winter sunset clutching your bedsheets.
10:28
18.05.17

Coloured Skirt

Where does contentment dwell? From droplets of juice that runnel down the table I watch the smiling of children kissing the cusps of cups, the intimate gazes tearing open the walls along the street dancing to distant salty lachrymose skips, I hear sorrow silenced, teeth grinding with dark thoughts hiding sadness inside. I sing out of tune with the cloud rhythms shaping horses, the lights return tired from the asphalt, dulled by the seductive coloured skirt on the corner.
17:06
03.06.17

Half-open Doorway

When the sun shines through the mountain range, shadows erect their tents on the asphalt where I lay my soul bare. I listen to the night-voice, so warming, saddened by my pale heart's panting, tea gulped down softening hairs stood on end, diminishing the taste of solitude. I howl at the wind, I bellow a river of cloud-couplets that block out the horizon with their horses and I sink my body into the drowsy dream-chair. The watcher's furious arpeggio at the rumbling passersby abandoning the building, crying inside, the unexpected gaze of an ageless crow on sleep's stoop. I drink the tea, I sweeten my tongue with images of the great wall and I decide it's night. In droves, the voices on the next floor dissipating the rage of barking dogs, I leave the cup to clink on the table free from infantile stripes and there I stay stock-still in the half-open doorway.

15:05
22.05.17

Feet

Feet shooting at glances obstructing the footpath. In the dream-yard the flights of birds stretch out. The crowd hides my reticence inside. Still expectant of fraternal shelter, my soles firmly planted in suicide's orbit. You can run with no purpose, bowing to shadows with no soul. Still radio-silence on nocturnal tasks, aches enamoured with fragile ankles. How to keep the hairs upright on the asphalt? The dull day drums, the tap spewing vital rivers, feet peeping bruises on the footpath.

15:06
29.05.17

Warm Tea

I cannot steal away the shadows spreading inside me. How fear and the unexpected play on the veranda of my introspections, delight in the errant dhow-boat fantasy where I navigate my destiny.
Waves salty skipping there on the margins of my vagrant self, insurging against the umbilical cord that lies on the algae-damp pavement.
Possible-self a martyr encloistered, an un-shelter covered in metaphysics, a rambler in orchards sprouting trucks of words so at nightfall the vermillion streaks obscuring my averted eyes don't break the secret doorway.
In darkness I harvest shadow fragments, the ones that conch my collided body with warm tea and Indian Ocean serenity.
20:32
30.05.17

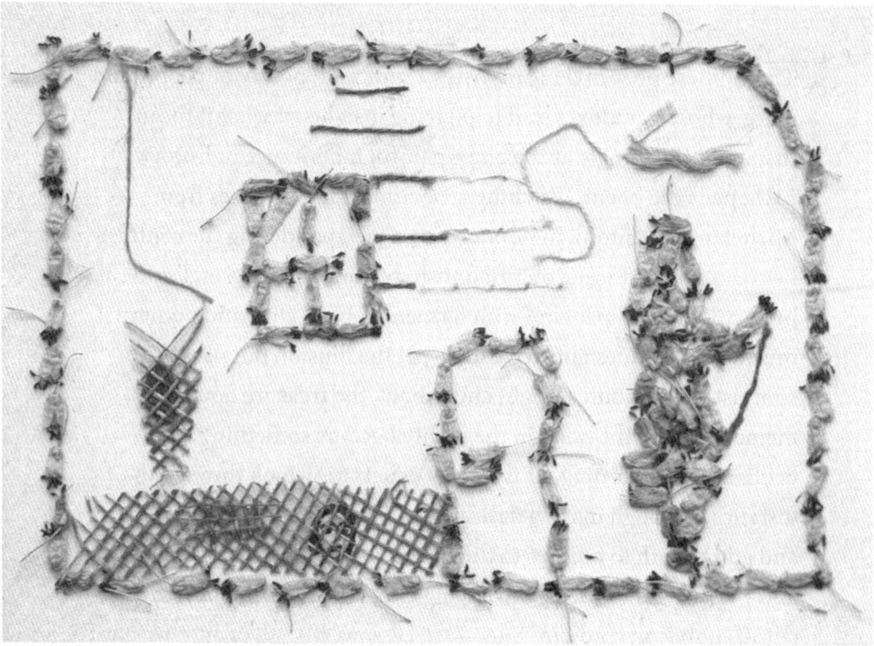

LIU LIGAN

Translated by Dong Li from Chinese

The Chinese poet LIU Ligan writes a profound poetry of people and place, whose paradoxes lead to piercing insights of what it means to look unflinchingly at the often-painful inheritance of history. LIU opens the poem 'Watching a Documentary—Scenes from Michelangelo Antonioni's *Chung Kuo, Cina*', pondering the contrast between a staged scene of 'ribbonfish, bream, and mackerel' and the hungry bellies of 'paofan / with fermented bean curd and potherb mustard'. LIU does not strive to dispel the illusion but uses the contrast to draw out 'a bright childhood', the treasure house of memory, where the holes in the reality become something 'brief, brilliant, like lightning'. It is by this penetrating look through the distance, 'through many a dawdling shadow', that memory animates and adds depth to our ties to the flawed people and things we love and that are gone, 'each glance tying another dead knot / on the cutoff umbilical cord'. In 'Literature Lesson', LIU gives another hard look at the storied past, 'a stifling long list' of 'the old literati / and their unanimous abandon', and asks a fundamental question of literature: whether writers should 'live in humility' for the sake of writing or die for dignity and honor while 'forsaking their talent and mission'. In the former residence of an 'overlooked 'decadent writer' who threw himself 'into a well / for ruined plants', the poet finds no answer but 'the tremendous legacy of silence'. It is this shivering silence that compels the poet to embark on this arduous road of literature. What is bequeathed to LIU is the resolve to speak against silence, and these two poems are powerful examples.

Watching a Documentary
—Scenes from Michelangelo Antonioni's *Chung Kuo, Cina*

1

    A crowded floating market,
    wooden springboards and boys' angular faces.
    Farmers scull and send over
    baby bok choy and letters with feathers.
    A wave of women workers wearing rubber aprons
    haul around baskets of ribbonfish, bream, and mackerel.
    Why on our table there is only paofan
    with fermented bean curd and potherb mustard?
    Alleyways crouch like skinny wildcats.
    A police tricycle carries a lady
    in a white dress around the corner.
    A flash of beauty,
    brief, brilliant, like lightning,
    and the eyes blinded for the moment
    blink still. It is the distant year of 1972,
    the black velvet of the night and the toy carriage
    with a broken spring. The frantic little cousin shrieks,
    licking a lollipop shaped as a precious pagoda,
    scampering and swinging the tapeworms
    in his split pants, as if a tail suddenly grows on him.
    Life is a bent shoulder pole,
    whose heavier end must be used
    to part the steam of the snack shop.
    And those who, by all means, want
    a bowl of noodles in the morning,
    blow their noses, forcing snot

and curse into their bellies.
And before it goes dark,
the boy running away from home returns,
with a torn smock, each hole
showing a bright childhood.
Antonioni's cunning montage
is taken to be evil. Such hostility
is not entirely without reason:
as in the temple, the clay Buddha's head
set to the stirring tunes of a model opera.

2

The shadow I cannot see
walks over the small stone bridge, the fraying
yellow schoolbag bouncing on the buttocks,
like grown-ups' doting pats.
The low eaves lower in the twilight,
like dissected fish scales, still busy
collecting baby teeth from the street.
In threes and fives, women arrive
at the riverbank to wash clothes, their wrinkles
dissolved into ancient ripples.
It is the same winding river
with mosses and the strange stench of ducks,
like a life to say goodbye,
like an endless loop of wool
for a custom-made shroud neatly folded
over the dowry at the bottom of the camphor chest.
There is so much love and death in this city,

you and me, you and them—
the shade reeling of summer heat,
the doorplates colored in rust, the lime walls
our eccentric neighbors cannot stop licking,
and the unquenchable thoughts
for the stove room and a bowl
of sugar porridge with lotus hearts.
But I can only love through the distance,
through the ghosts in the fog.
When the camera pulls away, the lights
come on, leaving the empty movie theatre
a complete mess and a row after another
of old seats with tattered velvet covers.
Once again, memories shrink
into dull images, shivering.
Common as a dog peeing under the tree,
as a bridge swarmed with tourists,
a stranger on the way home passes
through many a dawdling shadow,
each glance tying another dead knot
on the cutoff umbilical cord.

Literature Lesson

Lao She sank in a lake. Fu Lei hanged himself.
Xiong Shili died of hunger strike. And Shen Congwen
turned to the study of ancient Chinese apparel.
This is a stifling long list, overwintering
like daffodils shriveled on a windowsill,
like garlic scapes shooting sickly leaves of another age.
Still a student, I read their works,
be it literature or philosophy. I was taught
 "literature is the study of humanity,"
serious, like a solid house on the cliffs
that escorted the convulsive tributaries
of Soviet literature and the velvet drapes
of Critical Realism. I remain baffled
by the ineffectualness of the old literati
and their unanimous abandon.
Their insight into human nature did no help
to cleave through thorns a level path for posterity.
Instead, they blended themselves and thickened
the haze of the dark times. There were merely
the appealing thunderbolts of Scar Fiction,
but nowhere to find the silent lightning that pierced
the iron curtains. Between labor camps and rice patties,
between blue-black ink and sharpened fast gears,
should writers live in humility
for all the things they aspire to write about,
or should they, forsaking their talent and mission,
refuse smeared plates and die?
In the prime of my youth, I used to be enamored
of Hemingway's tough-guy novels, until the heroes

soon became as commonplace as chin beards.
As I began to contemplate the issues
of responsibility, literary actions, and such,
by sheer chance, I was led to a house
on a side street near Grandfather's,
the former home of an overlooked "decadent writer."
In my literary lectures, the Mandarin Ducks
and Butterflies School was just bonsais that added
colors to life. The idea of throwing oneself into a well
for ruined plants seemed nearly doubly absurd.
On that afternoon, in that deserted garden,
I suddenly came to understand
that only Zhou Shoujuan's death
could be called the true death of literature,
along with all the mundane, trivial,
insignificant disillusions of beauty, and the threads
pulled from the cocoons of the heart,
and the shattered souls of freedom
on the hastily stitched banners, and a blunt pen
breaking in the clamor of the eunuch's song.
From that moment on, I knew what I was inheriting
would be a tremendous legacy of silence.
When a whole generation of writers
turned into ghosts, unable to drown or starve any longer,
whether I pick up the pen as a rebel
or succumb to life for the sake of the written word,
I am doomed to fall into a fated,
incongruous vortex: sort of similar
to the hopeless shiver of a patient with Parkinson's,
to the bewildered stare, as tedious
as a lengthy conversation oscillating

between questions, as somber
as the folds of an ancient lady's undergarment
and the eternal speechlessness around the skull.

Note: Lao She was a novelist who was tortured during the Cultural Revolution and was said to have drowned himself. Fu Lei was a translator and critic who was persecuted at the beginning of the Cultural Revolution and committed suicide. Xiong Shili was an essayist and philosopher who was subjected to physical abuse at the beginning of the Cultural Revolution. Shen Congwen was a writer slated to win the first Nobel Prize in Literature for a Chinese writer but died before he could be awarded the prize. Zhou Shoujuan was a representative writer of the escapist Mandarin Ducks and Butterflies School, who threw himself into a well during the Cultural Revolution.

CLAUDE GAUVREAU

Translated from French by Carlos Lara

The Megalomanic Shields is the perfect example of what Gauvreau coined as '*exploréen*' language. At turns absurd, banal, and purely sonic, Gauvreau deploys glossolalia and neologism in eruptive, yet still legibly narrative, what I will call 'almost-sonnets'. The series' liberal composition advocates for an even more liberal translation: one can do almost anything to a language to which almost everything has already been done. What holds these poems together is their warm-bloodedness, their forceful thrust into a half-discernable existence. Their energy reads itself off the page. As one who rarely transliterates, I took the opportunity that these poems afforded to focus on translating their evocativeness, their verve. 'Shields' both block and expose, defend and attack. Here, we have poems, shields of megalomania, esoteric screens that occlude one meaning and then elucidate another. Having this flexibility to work with, I felt totally at ease in a language of which I still have a minimal grasp. *The Megalomic Shields* is truly an intermodal poetry in which meaning and feeling grapple passionately for the reader's attention.

from *The Megalomanic Shields*

Officer Threehouses
I am reborn on the bosom of pedutualbagzies
The ornaments
       have massacred
          the teals of round puzhess
It is a month
when the teeth of the tomb
have hung on their sigtal the pre-canine charcoal
Ovoz ovoxy

Cosmonauts have earthen brethren
And the judgment of mares comes from the bells that have inhaled the
          departure of the tutor
Hajjglombsick
The gazes of killers loved by the Papacy hop the maliciousfoof of the
          fools with watermelon forks
Long live the Geûnauzie!

The lousyman by pocketrider has blown away by the sides of the dike
    the worked tiles that we had deported from the cove
Crime has grooms who aspire to throw up the oath of the atheist
We will be there
Our dromedary will be disemboweled upon the wages of the unjust
I live And they die
Noutaboufe

Staligusta of carukedey of ascetic glandista
The igloohires have palomax
beyond the too-green of the trivanute maximalasses
Ogléhojéba
Aglistibozbastian of the praglingues to the statrissites schtaluples
The beak with stellar hormones walks on the waves of the present like
    a wandering cable
I am the god of the da-duvey durvy breeze
And my cassonte is the jibber jabber of the slain fugitive

DANTE ALIGHIERI

Translated by Philip Terry from Italian

My version of *Dante's Inferno*, relocated to the University of Essex, came out in 2014, and the sequel, *Dante's Purgatorio*, in 2024. Both are experiments with translation, simultaneously transtemporal and topographical, changing the time and the place of Dante, relocating it to contemporary Essex, and substituting Belfast, where I was born, for Dante's strife-torn Florence.

It was relatively easy to find contemporary equivalents for the *Inferno*'s villains; the more positive emphasis of the *Purgatorio* was more challenging – we live in a culture more at home with dystopias than utopias. Another challenge was the inescapable fact that the island of Purgatory was a mountain, and Essex is flat. I resolved this by setting the action on Mersea Island – at least Essex has its islands – in a parallel world, where climate artists have constructed a mountain out of Flexible Rock Substitute (FRS). Now I'm feeling my way into the *Paradiso,* from which the following extract is taken. Here one problem I encountered was the fact that Dante and Beatrice literally travel to the planets together, meeting the souls in Paradise— this seemed unfeasible in a contemporary version, so I decided to locate my poem firmly on earth. So in this extract rather than visiting the moon, Dante and Beatrice (here myself and Marina Warner) visit the restaurant Hello My Moon in Brighton. In Dante we meet the shades of nuns, Piccarda Donati and Empress Constance, who have been forcibly taken from their convents; I substitute more recent cases of abduction.

Dante's Paradiso III

As the carpet that had become a wing
Now came to rest, softly,
            outside Hello My Moon in Brighton,

I now saw how daft I'd been to take Marina
      so literally when she had said:
           "Now I'm going to fly you to the moon…"

Before I could open my mouth,
      and before I could take a look at the
Menu on the wall, she stood up and went straight in,

Greeting the waitress abruptly, I thought,
      but as she took a seat at a window table,
I caught her eye, and was about to say "OK, I get it,"

When right there, in front of my eyes, a vision
Appeared, absorbing my attention so absolutely
That all thought of talk left my mind.

As a fleeting image comes back to us of our own
Face reflected as we walk past a pane of glass in a
Bus shelter, or peer into the waters of a clear pond

Replete with goldfish, shallow enough for the bottom
To remain visible – a thing so faint that our eyes could
As soon make out a pearl necklace on a white T-shirt –

DANTE ALIGHIERI

Just such faces I saw there, eager to speak to me.
The second I became aware of them, believing them
to be reflected forms, I turned to find out who

They were, but saw nobody at all.
(I had made the opposite mistake to that made by
Narcissus as he gazed into the pool at his own double.)

Catching the eyes of my sweet guide again,
She smiled at me, radiantly, then whispered, sotto voce:
"You shouldn't be surprised to see me smile at your

Reaction, you dolt, you don't trust the evidence of your
Own senses; then you whirl round and stare at emptiness;
These are *real substances* that you see now,

Appearing here because their lives were cut short.
Speak to them, they are all citizens of the
Free State of Brighton, which is part of Paradise,

And when you have spoken to them, give your ears
To what they have to say in return, for they are incapable
Of deceit and they will tell you only what is true."

I turned then towards that shade who seemed to be
most eager to speak, and opening my mouth,
I began, moved by an unstoppable urge, to say:

"Ah, well-created spirit, who in these rays of continuing
Life enjoy that sweetness which, until tasted,
Can never be known,

How chuffed I'd be if you were so kind as to tell me
Who you are and tell me something about yourself."
Immediately, with smiling eyes, she said:

"In our world we cannot say no to a just request.
Before I ended my days in Hoad's Wood,
I worked as a marketing executive in digital media.

If you search your memory, you'll probably recall
A woman who was kidnapped near Clapham Common
By an off-duty police officer – Sarah Everard. That's me.

I'm here in Hello My Moon with a bunch of like-minded
Spirits whose lives were unfulfilled through no fault of their
Own. Since we died we've turned the other cheek,

And we rise above those who wronged us like air.
Our station might seem lowly to you – for sure, it's not
The greatest restaurant in town, but hey, check out

Our reviews on Tripadvisor – they're all 5-star –
And we're in Brighton, you could end up in worse places.
This is where we are and we like it here."

I said: "Your faces shine so brightly with something
Totally out-of-this-world that it alters you from how you
Once appeared, making my memory short-circuit,

But what you say reminds me of that terrible story,
And now I find it easy to recall your face. But tell me,
Are you happy here, in this restaurant, you don't

DANTE ALIGHIERI

Wish for somewhere a bit more upmarket?"
She smiled gently, as did the others gathered there,
then her words came, glowing with happiness:

"Brother, we're happy where we are, this place does
The best toasties in town, and if we want to pop
Out to another restaurant there's nothing to stop us.

We have the whole of Brighton at our fingertips,
And if we need a change we can take a trip abroad,
Gatwick's only just up the road. Look, we're in

Paradise, what more could we want? Everyone's
Equal here, and every place in it, whether it looks a bit
Down-at-heel to you or not, has equal worth."

Then it was clear to me that everywhere in
Paradise is Paradise, though sometimes the lights
Shine more brightly in one place than in another.

As happens when we've had our fill of one food, but
Still find we have appetite for other items on the menu,
And thanking the waitress as she whisks off one dish

Ask her to bring us another to follow, so did my words
And gestures beg to hear more of the circumstances
In which her all-too-brief life had come to its abrupt end.

"I was so happy that day," she said. "I'd been to visit a friend near
Clapham Common, and was making my way home on foot,
Almost skipping, when a policeman approached me.

At first I thought he was going to check if I was alright, but
He flashed his warrant card, then put handcuffs on me,
Which I immediately thought was strange.

He muttered something about breaking lockdown rules,
Then took me to a parked car and told me to get in.
He said he'd have to take me down the station.

I never saw the station. He drove for hours in darkness,
Barely talking, and when I protested he threatened
To hit me. Eventually we stopped outside some low

Building. He told me to get out, and took me inside.
That's when he raped me, and took my life away.
I can't tell you what happened afterwards, I wasn't there.

This other sister who shines so brightly beside me,
Here to my right, whose smiling face is so full with the light
That is radiant everywhere you look in our orbit,

Knows only too well from her own experience what I'm
Talking about. This shade found herself in such a state
Of depression following the death of her sister, that she

Turned to heroin to numb the grief. Then to pay for it
She turned to sex work. She was living in a hostel in
Glasgow at the time she disappeared, one night in 2005.

Her naked body was found five weeks later, in Limefield
Woods, near Biggar, South Lanarkshire. As always where
Sex workers are involved, the police dragged their feet.

Her killer, Iain Packer, a serial rapist, wasn't caught until
2024. She is the light of Emma Caldwell. She has known
No greater happiness than that of Hello My Moon."

These were the words she spoke, and then she started
To sing "Blue Moon", and singing this, she disappeared
As something sinking in deep waters fades,

And I, who had been so fixed upon her bright form
Until the moment she suddenly vanished, turned round
And set my eyes once more on that other radiance –

In Marina's face now was I all-absorbed –
But her luminosity flashed so deep into my overstrained
Retinas that I could not bear the sight, so at first I

Found it difficult to put any questions to her.

MIMI HACHIKAI

Translated from Japanese by Eric E. Hyett and Spencer Thurlow

Mimi Hachikai won the Japanese government's 56th annual 'Emerging Artists' Encouragement Prize' for her 2006 book, *Tonight We Are Predators*. The book's Japanese title 食う物は食われる夜 (kuumono wa kuwareru yoru), means literally, 'the night when things that eat get eaten'.

As translators, we felt a gravitational urge toward this work due to its unique subject matter: a reversal of the natural food chain, radical empowerment of small creatures, and exploration of prehistoric and vestigial human feelings. From the very beginning, our trusted circle of English-language readers let us know that Ms. Hachikai's poetry was working for them.

The speaker in 'Early Asiatic' might easily be one of Ms. Hachikai's pre-Japanese ancestors. Someone possessed of the modern skills of hunting and cooking, yet still coming to terms with the reality of being human. Someone both embracing and questioning her animal nature.

The very enjoyable love poem 'Automated Mollusc' contains many clues that could steer the reader toward a sexual interpretation. Under that reading, the clam evokes a metaphor for female anatomy and pleasure. The last stanza in particular reads beautifully with a more sexual undertone.

At the same time, the poem is very theatrical: 'windows are just stage sets / actual views are also stage sets'. Also there is a great amount of clam-specific imagery, the animal itself with eyes at the waterline. So we leave it to the reader to interpret!

Early Asiatic

I slurp
alone at midday
both palms on the grass
chewing the charred   well-done   meat
that falls from the bone
soon enough separates
between my teeth
the fire   drunk dry
I lift my fingers
to the embers

Automated Mollusc

I wait five days   for your reply
no good after the bite
when I'm face-to-face with feathered things
lines with no shadow,   recognizable
in my retinas   the afterglow of things   settling down
[you]   are always that way
arms folded you escape   anyone's eyes
and occupy the impossible seat
next to to the concept of cause and effect
that which rises   instantly into anxiety and   pleasure
(I guess)

What you see
is no mistake
[my]   way   is far more unique
cutting and pasting in various sizes
page   after page   I carry my extravagance
atop my head   from near   and far
so if something strange happens,   no worries
logic's jumping needle   has a falling timbre
that strikes my eardrums   day and night
weaving   while expanding round-the-clock's
stitched pattern   don't worry   it happens
(it happens a lot)

[you] can't forgive [me]
for leaving the musical score
I can bathe in the undisguisable disgust   in the lenses of your glasses
we're standing   water-soaked bushes budding
and [you]   unable to accept   differences
Still,   [I] want to taste the grass   of the road
and the grass of one springtime   after another
I want   the fieldsong   of picking greens,
abundance rising up the stem
(starting to blur)
I share my gloomy outlook: our
hierarchy (is a monkey cage) where everyone
can be torn   apart   and eaten   in comfortable silence.
things won't be so bad in   the (everyday)   leaves of speech
I would like to speak with [you]
despite our differing directions   and hopes
but even if I could see your hope
exchange hopes
you'd say nothing.

My eyes, so terribly dry just above the water level
they tear   a line through the landscape from the edge
where sky meets sea   melts helplessly into a dividing line
a floating tower mirage   vertical and horizontal
with a rusted, cracked shriek of a siren
everyone flinches   when worked over   by expert hands
that's   our clam spirit
never resting until we've   seen it through
the mythical mollusc

moves a little bit
crushed spirit
carved out   for later
shut the lid and take a little rest
windows   are just   stage sets
actual views   are also stage sets
won't you send the answers that do not come
they exist   they're perhaps
in the cupboard   that dull slow drawer
third from the bottom
won't you lift those low-power
binoculars to both eyelids,
squint and look for them

I wait five days   for your reply
no good after the bite
when I'm face-to-face with feathered things
the tower of water has begun to weaken
shake the mythical mollusc   with all your might
bury your head in the mythical mollusc's sleeping breath
until it awakens
in these binoculars: *hey*
what in the world is that?

STÉPHANE BOUQUET

Translated from French by Matt Reeck

Being interested in form, I was immediately taken by Bouquet's *Dans l'année de cet âge* (All That Was That Year) because of its way of combining two types of chronicle poems—the one, minimalist; the other, maximalist. While I may have in passing described the minimalist ones as haiku-like poems, in truth, they defy the haiku's mannerist way of looking at the world; instead, they offer short poems of striking directness while lying outside of a learned metaphysics of perception. They are mundane, and yet by finding the mundane capable of 'speaking' to our deepest interests (in other words, when we notice something we give value to it), they become part of our fragile quest for transcendence. These short poems are then expanded in a long form (the notes), which are at the back of the book, and so a bibliophilic reading habit grows in flipping back and forth over the pages, seeing how the kernels first laid in the ground bloom into fully formed descriptions and stories. Due to the fact that the title comes from ancient customs for cenotaph inscriptions, there is then added emphasis laid on discovering the full life underneath the pithy stele. And because there is a person's curious encounters with his morbid consciousness on display in this book, this toggle between the stele and the story becomes that much more interesting and exciting.

from *All That Was That Year*

10. Poem for two couples

In this slow mountain train
There are two couples on vacation
No doubt ecstatic to be up among
the fresh grass the air the peaks

I imagine a clear mountain lake
and how they will say in their ecstasy
how beautiful it all is[1]

---

[1]. To get to Gap, I had to change trains in Grenoble. The next was a slow one that wound down through the Alps. I can't tell you any longer what parts of the landscape sent me into raptures: no doubt it was the breaches between mountains where the sky rushed in and then the mountains on the horizon; the sheath of clouds around a summit; things like that: the alpine scenery, the last snow patches, once in a while the deep blue of a mountain lake. Truth be told, I think I was mostly thinking about the summers long ago when my mother and I used to go places like this to climb the trails, do the intermediate peaks, anticipate the final bend around which the lake, the glacial waters, the purity of the world (I used to imagine) (she used to say) would surge forth. In the train, there were two couples—a man and a woman each time—holding hands, leaning toward each other, laughing, talking, kissing, wanting much more than that. They were going to Briançon (as, I remember, my mom and I did one summer). I couldn't make myself believe that they were going there for anything other than what we had done: we took long walks, we climbed up the mountain once in a while, she would tell me not to run, she would take my backpack (as well as carrying her own) for little stints; she would tell me that it was just there, right ahead, just maybe four more turns: I believed her. And then it was right there, the enchanted (she said) blue mirror of the lake where I would see my reflection.

11. *Poem for one of the four*

I also imagine
on the train's slow climb up
if I was to fall begging to my knees in front of one of the four
which it would be[2]

---

[2]. The two couples continued their coupling activities (within the limits of decency). One of the four was my favorite. He wore printed, blue pants of a light fabric; the print was dark blue on white. His hair wasn't necessarily in the best taste either, but he clearly took a special pleasure in running his hands through its healthy mass. I wasn't thinking anything that specific (suck him off, or him me; fuck him up the ass, or him me). I think it was the way he looked so shockingly middle-class that excited me. I wanted to know what it would have looked like to have our two bodies next to each other, and how they would have made love.

12. Poem for a path

I write the
Poem of the Mountain
up here
in the alpine promontories of the South

I walk higher to remain faithful to the poem

I write that the mountain is deserted and desolate
flattened by the heat and that the storm has found me
but it's a lie   I'm alone here[3]

3. I was walking above Gap. Despite the heat and my fatigue, which had struck suddenly from who knew where, I continued to climb higher and higher. I've always liked routes leading to solitude and nothingness. On these climbs, each time, the city grows further away, and then I can see beyond its outskirts (suburban warehouses in aluminum, hay fields, wheat or rye fields, the highway). The heat was intense, I was dead tired: I kept fighting off the urge to turn back. But I was writing this so-called poem of the mountain, and the credibility of literature hung in the balance: I had to continue since the poem said that I was. Finally, I got to the top: nothingness and sky saturated black.

[A previous version of this poem included two other lines:
> I didn't have any separation to bear witness to
> nor love to regret

These were hyper-precise allusions to the "Poem of the Mountain," which Marina Tsvetaeva had written after a separation while looking back wistfully on a lost love. I used to love this poem, and especially her audacity, and how she would compact meaning in the unspoken, and how she would make sounds bounce off one another (at least in the translations of Ève Malleret). But I got rid of these two lines: they were clumsy allusions, and they lengthened the poem for no reason, if the poem would have been able to accommodate this detour: it was a mountain path with cutbacks through the grass and rocks, I wasn't going directly into the nothingness and the black sky.]

13. Poem for easing fear

A childhood memory of a sudden trampling of leaves
The beast sprang
and my mother screamed to warn me

If the dog that time
had dug its canines into my throat
what would I ever have penned
but an unexpected Poem of My Death[4]

---

4. It's another day, the next day, most likely. I was hiking on a very straight path through a stifling forest that ran alongside a long ditch which would almost certainly be filled with water in winter. Gradually, the path became less well-marked (on the ground, it was clear that the number of hikers there was dwindling: they doubted that the path really went anywhere, and feared getting lost in the mountains and the dense forest: gradually, in short, the forest was closing in). I could hear the sounds of animals (birds) in the green enclosure. I thought back to the huge crazy dog that had raced up on us (one summer day) and would have killed us if its owner hadn't called it off in time. My mother had called out to me in warning, and she was ready for it, she had barred its way and was ready to die for me. I walked away terrified that it would show up again, and that feeling continued all the way till the end of the path, but now my mother is no more. [In the Tsvetaeva I have that is published by L'Âge d'Homme, "Poem of the Mountain" is followed by "The End." I don't think it's about death (I'm not sure though), but my poem is a sort of continued invisible homage. Invisible: Yaël Pachet, who knows Tsvetaeva's work well, didn't see anything about M. T. in these poems when (on my request) she read them.]

JUAN CARLOS BUSTRIAZO ORTIZ

Translated from Spanish by Ben Bollig and Mark Leech

Juan Carlos Bustriazo Ortiz (1929–2010) was born in Santa Rosa, in the Argentine province of La Pampa. With only a sixth-grade education, his literary knowledge was almost wholly autodidactic. He wrote his first poems aged twelve and in his twenties was part of a local music and poetry scene. Bustriazo lived an itinerant life in the open spaces of La Pampa. His nomadism and Buenos Aires' centrality to literary life in Argentina meant he never found a space within the national poetry scene. Much of his writing is rooted in his poetic wandering lifestyle, featuring characters and stories he encountered, often in bars, many of which are on no map. Rural Argentina's indigenous folklore and cosmology run through his poetry too. Bustriazo owned almost no possessions, except a drinking cup and a portfolio containing his life's work, which was once lost, supposedly at the house of a female friend. He published little and earnt scant recognition, and only in his last years enjoyed (limited) artistic fame, partly through devotees such as poet and editor Cristian Aliaga. An outsider and a rebel, Bustriazo has become a cult figure in Argentina, particularly since his death.

Bustriazo's poetry leaps from genre to genre, with a liberal sprinkling of neologisms. To re-imagine his style(s) into English we had to follow his lead beyond conventional 'sense'. Our collaboration is a melding of two verse translations, one with a deep grounding in the language (Ben), and one exploring the poems' experimental potential in English (Mark). In bringing them together we hope both Bustriazo's words and itinerant spirit will travel to new worlds.

OPUS TRISTILUS

today I came out of my cavern love it was raining pollen I want to say a strange thing first well I didn't know it surprised me shocked me it fell from the greysonic sky something on my incredulous back on my quaternary shoulders on my chest with lizards on my member's violet skin like an absurd dog I drew closer to the face of these unknown threads and they were yellowy so intense made me tremble and gooseflesh they made me solitude that was before the rain of water because first it rained pollen my love because it was pollen that rained this evening when dark was falling anointment grew in the heaping-up of the night and from a high cosmic tree it rained pollen my love it rained pollen and in hananolida's house too the pollen fell and she thought of her womb and in nurma's house too and she thought of her womb and in ascuala's house too and she thought of her womb and in salila's house too and she though of her womb and in chilona's house too the pollen rained and she thought of her womb then I knew it was true my love after it rained water and I didn't believe

(temple, 4.)

Saintfire 10

Saintfire of the moonmountain
saintfire I knew and don't know.
Things from there, Ataliva,
once on the road with, you know.

A fire used to walk with me.
It was a walker just like me
and a drinker of the night
turned to caldén and in bloom.

In the leaves it was kindling.
The spell was singing aloud
and the song was open wide
as if enmooned and crackling.

Vermillion bo'l

3.
and we tried to blow water back
where the round mud is trod
but it smiled like a mirror
so ladylike the sleeping water
the hips it had blue and black
the black navel clearing
we tried to look for people
they'd made themselves wings like smoke
we tried to rescue those breads
those ingots of dark work
that unwove without one oh
into threads of green mud
we wanted to save the roof
the ceiling beams had collapsed
the piquillin shrubs window panes
that smiled brokeluckily
muddily a magpie passed
with a pink little worm
I don't know if sun will come back one day
I don't know if she'll go down one day

5.
and in the burners they lit fire
and the people danced sleepwalking
the pyramids stumps mulberries
of crusted pale-lit loaves
and the dry berries danced
from the reddened soft fruit
so much in music entwined
so much gazing in each's eyes
the moaner danced lightly
and called you among brambles
and blue bugs danced
great vermillion butterflies
danced the dust of the earth
the breeze all harnessed up
and very night the kiss was made
and hips were wounded
waists were scuffed up
in the sweeping spellmaking
green lightning you didn't come down
nor all empurpled were you me!

'Compelling and curious'

Sasha Dugdale on Kim Hyesoon

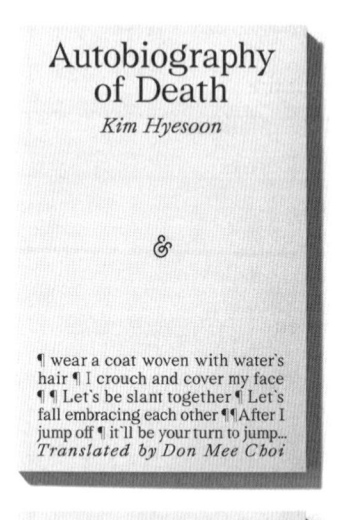

Autobiography of Death
Kim Hyesoon

¶ wear a coat woven with water's hair ¶ I crouch and cover my face ¶ ¶ Let's be slant together ¶ Let's fall embracing each other ¶ ¶ After I jump off ¶ it'll be your turn to jump...
Translated by Don Mee Choi

Winner of the Griffin International Poetry Prize

Winner of the Lucien Stryk Asian Translation Prize

Phantom Pain Wings
Kim Hyesoon

¶ This book is not really a book ¶ It's an I-do-bird sequence ¶ a record of the sequence ¶ ¶ When I take off my shoes. stand on the railing ¶ and spread my arms with eyes closed ¶ feathers poke out of my sleeves ¶ Bird-cries-out-from-me-day record ¶ I-do-bird-day record ¶ as I caress bird's cheeks... *Translated by Don Mee Choi*

Winner of the 2024 National Book Critics Circle Award for Poetry

2024 Poetry Book Society Translation Choice

'Otherworldly spaces.' THE NEW YORKER

And Other Stories

Sign up to And Other Stories monthly newsletter for details of Kim Hyesoon and Don Mee Choi's UK tour in June.

@andotherpics | @andothertweets | @andotherbooktok | andotherstories.o

Finally published in the UK & Europe

March — **Hardly War** — *Don Mee Choi*

¶ I was born in a tiny, traditional, tile-roofed house, a house my father bought with award money he received for his photographs of the April 19, 1960 Revolution. The student-led revolution overthrew the authoritarian South Korean president, Syngman Rhee, installed by the US government in 1948. He tells me even elementary school students came out to join high school and college students in protest, their arms locked shoulder to shoulder.

April — **DMZ Colony** — *Don Mee Choi*

¶ ... return ... return ... return ... return ... return ... return ...
¶ ... return ... return ... return ... return ... return ... return ...
¶ ... return ... return ... return ... return ... return ... return ...

May — **Mirror Nation** — *Don Mee Choi*

¶ The westerly wind blows across a patch of desert outside my apartment window facing north: the Deutschlandradio, the ever-spinning ring of Mercedes-Benz, and the metal fences set up for the construction of new housing. Only the fences remind me of home—the endless barbed wire across the waist of a nation. A cooler temperature expected this morning before the heat wave arrives tomorrow. On 28.6.1950, in Seoul, three days after the war had begun, my father washed his face and looked up at the stars on a clear night, then decided to head out to the city center.

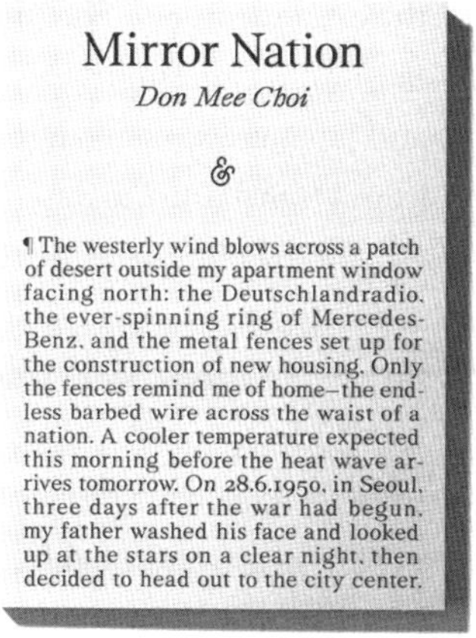

First UK publication for the unmissable, interdisciplinary Korea-USA trilogy by the 2020 National Book Award for Poetry winner

And Other Stories

Sign up to And Other Stories monthly newsletter for details of Kim Hyesoon and Don Mee Choi's UK tour in June.

@andotherpics | @andothertweets | @andotherbooktok | andotherstories.org

CHIKA SAGAWA

Translated to and from Japanese and English
by Sawako Nakayasu and Megumi Moriyama

For some time now I have been working with the Japanese poet, critic, and translator Megumi Moriyama on a series of investigations and experiments in which we act as both poet and translator, entwining the two roles. Moriyama and her sister, co-translator Marie Mariya, are famous (and perhaps even notorious) in Japan for their translation back into Japanese of Arthur Waley's original translation into English of Murasaki Shikibu's *The Tale of Genji*, the world's first novel. At the same time, I had been translating the poems of Chika Sagawa, a previously unknown, now 'established' modernist poet, in both conventional and unconventional ways. As poetry-translation collaborators, I dare say that we were meant for each other.

Our current project is an investigation of poetry translation in the expanded field. Starting with translations of the poems of Chika Sagawa, we are simultaneously writing and translating, with English and Japanese as core languages. Moriyama and Mariya use the term 'spiral translation' to describe translation that is less linear, more welcoming of possibilities that spiral out of the original. This current series of poems we are sharing begins with an original poem in Japanese by Chika Sagawa, which gives clues to Sagawa's own multilingualism: it includes a French title, 'Promenade' (the Japanese orthography alerts us to its French origin), as well as the English word 'screen'. The next poem is a conventional translation, which is followed by a multilingual, multi-format trajectory that includes the introduction of some in the form of Japanese haiku. The English translation of haiku engenders new decisions and definitions around that particular form.

In this process of translating across language, form, and historical contexts, the only thing we regret is that Sagawa herself is unable to join us.

プロムナアド
By Chika Sagawa (左川ちか)

季節は手袋をはめかへ
鋪道を埋める花びらの
薄れ日の
午後三時
白と黒とのスクリイン
瞳は雲に蔽はれて
約束もない日がくれる

Promenade

*Translated into English by Sawako Nakayasu
from Chika Sagawa's Japanese*

Seasons change their gloves
The three o'clock
Trace of sun
Of flower petals that bury the pavement
A black and white screen
Eyes are covered by clouds
Evening sets on some promiseless day.

Promenade (C)

By Sawako Nakayasu based on Chika Sagawa's Japanese

Seasons remplace   gloves

      fading light

three o'clock

      flowers fill the nouvelles

a black and white screen

      eyes

           covered by clouds at

the end of a day   sans

                  promise

プロムナアド　　*Promenade (H-haiku)*

森山恵　による　ナカヤスサワコ　による　左川ちか
By Megumi Moriyama based on Sawako Nakayasu's English
based on Chika Sagawa's Japanese

ぬぎ交わす春手袋サワコ　ちか

桜蘂ちる敷石へ錆びたナイフ

黒衣の花盗びと麻酔の夕べ

Promenade (H-haiku)

Translated to Sawako Nakayasu's English from Megumi Moriyama's Japanese based on Sawako Nakayasu's English based on Chika Sagawa's Japanese

Exchanging and removing the gloves of spring – Megumi, Chika

Cherry blossom, stamen, pistil – fall to the pavement, where a rusty knife

Sheathed in black, a theft of flowers, evening insensate

DANA RANGA

Translated from German by Christina Hennemann

I first discovered Dana Ranga's collection 'Hauthaus' (meaning 'house of skin') as a reader. I was struck by how effortlessly she moves between poetry and prose, crossing boundaries and bending genres. Ranga's prose poems were a unique reading experience for me. I was fascinated by musicality and precision in her work. The collection these poems are taken from explores the human body and travels through its organs, revealing stories of trauma, love and resilience, and tapping into the broader scope of immigration, religion, and politics. Her poems paint intimate connections between the physical and emotional realms.

   Translating 'Liver' and 'Spleen' presented several challenges due to the intricate interplay of word choice, syntax, imagery, and cultural context. These prose poems rely on linguistic subtleties and idiomatic expressions that are unique to the German language. Another difficulty lay in conveying the rhythm and musicality inherent in Ranga's writing. The flow of her prose, characterised by its cadence and use of sound devices such as alliteration and assonance, contributes greatly to the reader's experience. Recreating these auditory elements in another language required creative adaptations while protecting the meaning of the original text.

   In translating Ranga's work, particularly her longer prose poems, I hope to convey their musicality and her unique voice, which is deeply rooted in her German-Romanian background and yet universally accessible. My translations are my attempt to contribute to a conversation about genre, language and crossing linguistic boundaries. It's been a rewarding experience to engage with Ranga's work as it has enriched my understanding of what poetry and language can achieve.

Liver

He's sitting there and lets her decay, is I-am really Being or just being his? – understand and don't stand up, she is said to have wanted it that way, it just scratches something so hoarse out of the voice, that's why they're flying against the window now, icy-the-wind, it throttles them and they only see light and off they go, black and light in a nosedive, down to the right, narrow, thin bundles, delicate, elastic sinews, pull inwards at an obtuse angle, plumage, hair erector, winter hasn't been this loud for a long time, the melody shatters, can one feel it in the now? – or just the breathing and holding on,

epibiotic organism with no home, what's the use of the splendour under the earth, arum, flamingo flower, bent or upright, with aerial roots one wears the open hair, salty and flaming, so one only asks, what-hurts-loudly, one syllable, nothing more, iced door lock, spoiled bread, the immeasurable, careless of above and below, to the left or to the right, circling around the illusion of twinkling stars, sucked up by the silence, and that for days, only then roots continue to grow, from head to pubis, on breast and bone, fear drives them into the I-am, expels the Is and avoids the Being, vola manus and planta pedis hairless, like fingertips and lips,

frozen and cracked, lock and face, for defence and decoration, horn fibres root in the skin, a greyed flock of birds, feather-star, and yet, it is his, soft light, in fact a shy song, forget the Where, asks further, one look back and Being becomes I-was, the first coat of hair always made of wool fibres, prenatal elegance, bristle-hair over the eyes, eyelashes on the lids, cilia, a rug in the auditory canal, a loud law, vector, draw the line, the stroke of the pen, he gets up, only after she the door, almost silently, out of consideration for the cold and the lock, what carries the immeasurable outside? – a point, as if the place was tangible, where one takes roots, no knife, no boiling water, no place to feed on the sounds, the baby chokes, down feather in the throat, four syllables only, he cries and falls silent, a question is allowed anything, even beyond the verdict, maybe someday, but nothing breaks off like I-am, the walls are wavering, they're shaking off the pictures, what has been seen and said penetrates through the cracks, the banging of the trowels, the voices of the masons, merely coal and wood consume themselves with lasting trace, with each broken tip nearer to the point, he-is,

      she-is, it begins, combing and parting, with a narrow hand, so much liking for the skin stretching over the knuckles, an intimated kiss, blue rivulets under the ice, hugging out of decency, the track feigns sacrifice, like a shaved head, and when smiling the lips stay shut, he counts the steps, she returns, as if the is wasn't hers, that way it's easier to carry, the swarming works, she faces him, the gaze erases the auxiliary lines, from one digit to another, over word-bridges, cast into sounds alive, after the comma the endless root of a number, eyelash by eyelash, shiny and black, a plait, braided from two strands, certainty attached to possibility, pinned up with a comb of bright horn—

Spleen

The show always begins on time, the sun is shining through the fins of the roller blinds, today there are eight gaps, yesterday there were twelve and today he wants to sleep in later, but in five minutes the lions on the telly will roar, the hunted suddenly turn around and take a swing, I have to see that, cut to the applauding monkeys, then a man with a gun will come to aid and hunt the hunting, opening credits, lots of names, also for lions and chimpanzees, for parrots and tarantulas, it's still a long way to the power switch, hundreds of shingles creaking parquet, and then I turn off the sound, to be on the safe side, so that the roaring doesn't reach the bedroom, one can only see it then, and the rustling of the trees,

    I slowly turn around, one leg is already on the edge of the bed, a lamb is waiting down below, and the blanket above me, eight kilograms of wool divided into two point five by two point five, for two people, it smells of cage and the sweat of the keepers, pets smell different, they are predictable, with tame mitochondria and transparent cell walls, breeds for fidelity and submission, for procreation, giving birth, raising, slaughtering and still no peep, no oh-alas, just march to bed, eyes closed and press on, last night as well, with the hope of tomorrow and the prospect of a world in black and white, eyes closed and through the middle of the night, guzzling the night, the darkness, moving only when he moves,

    waiting until he falls asleep, then slowly crawling out from under the blanket, on hands and feet around the bed, turning down the volume on his radio, mixing night into the wavelengths, muting the chirp of space, with a canon, inhale-exhale, women's voices and men's voices and always the same, at this time it's always war, always uprising and rebellion and punishment with death, turn the volume down, then switch off, wait, until the *click* drowns in his cough, and then back, the same way, on the same parquet shingles, the solid and quiet ones, now it's quiet, like in space, when all the life-sustaining devices fail at the failure of the power generator, and now back to the edge of the bed, hated spaceship, because I have to share it, and don't slide in his direction, in the deep ditch where he's sleeping and sweating and sometimes mumbles and talks, turn-the-radio-on-again, I want to listen to the three-o'clock-news, and falls back into the moor of dreams, radio antennas growing tall and making the darkness's blood surge, wet pillows and rough sheets, last night prisoners were exchanged, with hissing and humming, it was too warm under the blanket, but it happened fast, in strictest secrecy, it's peeping and whistling, the lamb on the edge of the bed lifts its head and searches in vain for its mother's teats, then it sinks into the hay and sleeps, quick on a sleep-journey, riding brain waves,

    there is a lot of green in black and white, happiness is brushing against the edge of the jungle and kills a gazelle, flesh and blood live and die at the same time, painless cut, cut to the next scene, everything is for the good in life, even the cage bars, because one can shake them, screeching, howling, the smile of the captured chimpanzees is a grimace, who is mirroring whom here, nothing is primitive, everything is as it is, legitimate, not legitimate, like the faces of the hunters in the makeup room, before shooting begins, the chimpanzee knows what a cage is, when she frees the parrots, a huge strike, little head and wings, freedom and the great guzzling are awaiting you, being eaten mostly, don't-be-afraid and so-what, that's life, God only gives what one can carry, the cage is small because one seemingly doesn't need that much, of space and freedom, the thoughts are content with just their own mind,

    how many years have to pass until the blind crumbles into dust, it is more powerful than light, and only when he says, now-you-can-get-up, does the night come to an end, and he speaks again, stay-put,

I-want-to-sleep-in, don't-make-a-noise, he rules day and night and three quarters of the bed surface,

    I flee to my quarter at the edge of the bed and sleep without a pillow, it's lying between us, my right foot is already out, the left follows and then a slight rotation of the axis to the right, until the big toe touches the lambskin, the springs remain silent, no quick movements and oh, were I amongst my own kind, in the black-and-white-forest, in the good-and-evil-world, in the world-of-justice, where the script presents death and every knuckle and cartilage of a striped, dotted, rainbow-colored enemy, and I rise up, towards the light, spread my wings, float over the parquet and touch down quietly, at the door, open and close it behind me, and then only the switching on, Sundays, always at ten past nine—

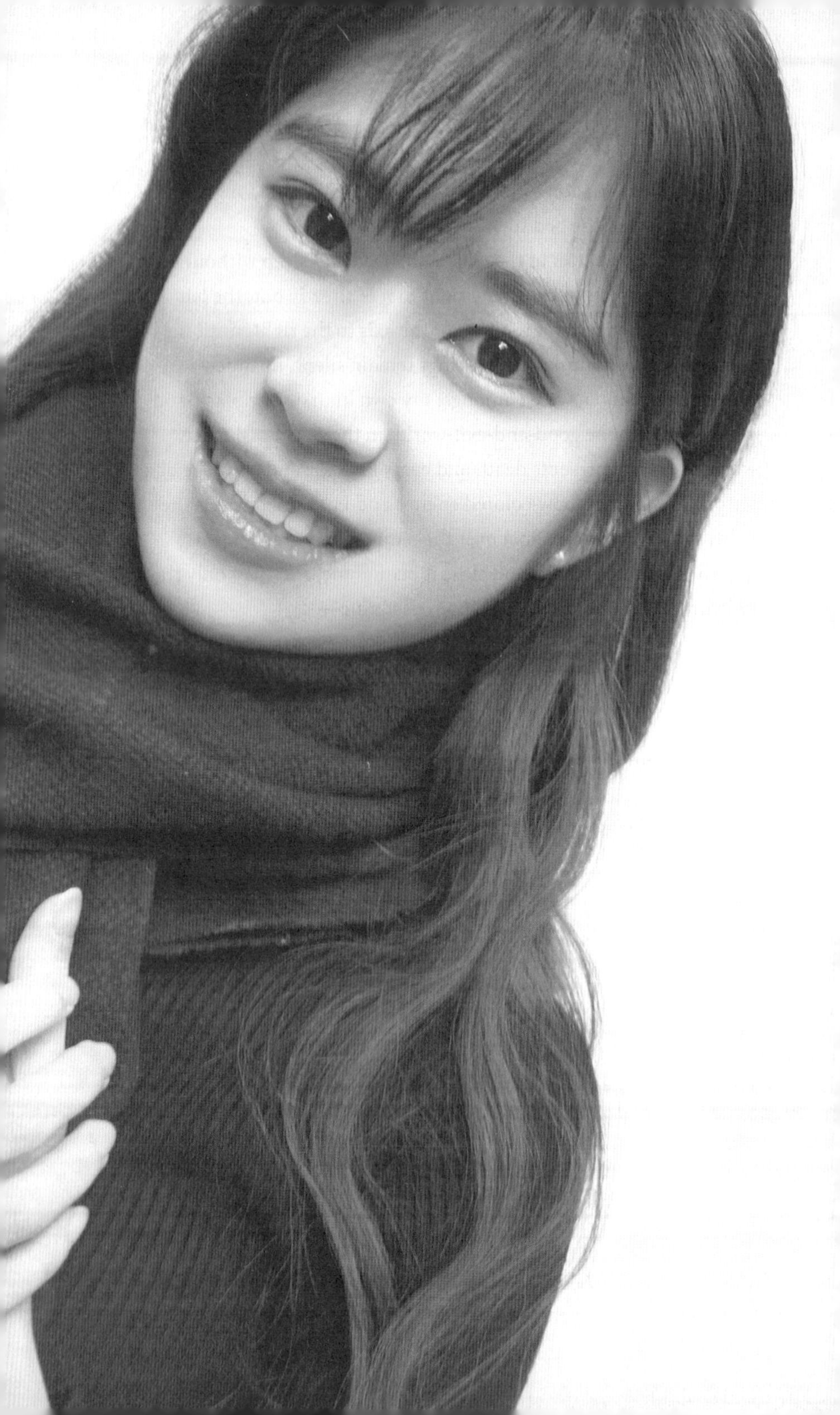

MOON BO YOUNG

Translated from Korean by Dabin Jeong

Moon Bo Young's BATTLEGROUND is about two women—SongKyungRyun and KangMingMing—in the world of a battle royale video game. As the two lovers figure out how to exist as 'two' in a world built for the 'last man standing', the identities and narratives of these two lovers unfold; at the same time, the dividing line between reality and game also begins to collapse.

BATTLEGROUND is a striking avant-garde poetry collection that integrates hybridity, drawings, polivocality, and a tender queer narrative into one bold conceptual framework, one that signifies the cultural influence of video games on literary works.

In translating BATTLEGROUND, my utmost goal was to distinguish the three voices—the narrator, SongKyungRyun, and KangMingMing—and to capture each point of view (POV, in in-game language). As the collection features 'characters' and is centered around the narrative developing between the characters—it being love or death—it felt crucial for the characters to speak through the poems written in their perspectives, such as in 'BATTLEGROUND—The One Who Fell into the Wall', where the speaker of the poem unabashedly says, 'I'm not uncomfortable with my greed'.

Another great focus in my translation of BATTLEGROUND was to make use of the creative freedom the manuscript provided me. Moon's language is extremely playful and she incorporates multimedia to present her unique imagination whole in her poetry, exemplified by the poem, 'BATTLEGROUND—The Happening Talks about Itself'. My translation reflects this hybridity, freely exploring the possibilities of Moon's imagination, in the hopes to welcome the readers into the world of BATTLEGROUND.

Opposite: Moon Bo Young

Battleground
—The One Who Fell into the Wall

Together, while passing through a wall
You disappear
It left an impression on me

Feeling like there are too many walls
Enumerate boredom
The one who fell into the wall

You disappeared
And to that, I reacted

I'm in the middle of a confrontation
The guy babbles in a foreign language
If I can't understand, it's impressive

If you're going to disappear, disappear more and reappear already

Whenever I see a wall I want to pull you out
And scare you

I am not uncomfortable with my greed

You want to keep staying there

Battleground
—The Happening Talks about Itself

KangMingMing: What is that on your waist?

SongKyungRyun: (Unbuttons the shirt to show the orange electrodes cross-mounted on her chest) A portable electrocardiogram machine.

KangMingMing: Put that away. It feels like something might happen.

SongKyungRyun: I put it on because something has already happened.

*

Diagnostic Assessment: Let's use the graph of a healthy human heart as our reference. Make a small human walk your ground.

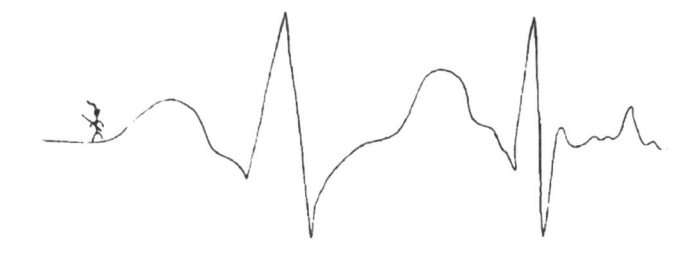

Let her observe the terrain for a minute and then observe the small human.

If the terrain has 68 sloughs to stumble, and 70 to 100 small but irritating jagged stones, and a giant mountain that requires a detour, in other words

If the small human stumbles 68 times, trips over and falls 70 to 100 times, and experiences a breakdown in front of a giant mountain that ignites her adventurous spirit but makes her practice surrender, in other words

If you could provide another person with an experience of ceaseless walking, you

Still have a beating heart.

*

An electrocardiogram records electrical changes in the human body, and if no one is tripping and falling that person is a dead person.

*

SongKyungRyun and KangMingMing are looking at the small human exploring the terrain. The small human is standing in front of a small pit. The duo talks while looking at the face of the small human. Look, KangMingMing is observing the dust on the portable electrocardiogram machine. If this scene seems beautiful, beauty is almost like a mistake.

ANGLO-SAXON POEMS (VARIOUS AUTHORS)

Mistranslated from Old English by Leo Boix

I began to view mistranslations as intricate linguistic processes that enabled me to explore meaning, syntax, and shifts in language when translating a poem from Spanish (my mother tongue) to English and occasionally back again. This involved experimenting with unusual sounds, rhymes, and flow as new versions emerged from the remnants. Mistranslations serve as a fitting metaphor for my cultural and linguistic journey as a migrant from Argentina to the UK. This experience has often led to misunderstandings and misrepresentations, much like many of my mistranslations. I considered mistranslated bodies, actions, and ideas, recognising that not everything can or should be translated and that meaning cannot always be fully grasped.

    I drew upon Anglo-Saxon poetry as a foundation, as these early forms of the English language provide a linguistic and stylistic starting point. They are frequently recognised for their alliteration, strong rhythm, and caesura, as well as their playful essence. By mistranslating these poems, which date from the 5th to the 12th centuries in the British Isles, I began to explore and interrogate themes of migration, diaspora, and displacement, which resonate with both Anglo-Saxon poetry and my own experiences.

from *The Exile's Lament*

I am barely a phantasm, a guy in a boat
                unwaved. I wander around with little.
I'm cold, a 35-year-old, and *oh friend*,
            gulp me as a sitting snail. I am a cross
in the ocean. Poverty is a plague, like me.
                Dennis is my deepest desire, and threesomes,
sex, the tall ones. In May, the good ones open
                like flowers, as your breast. It is late,
find me in the city—soon I will be 40.
            A butt I bear (behind), slender and sensual.
Hold my column, my characteristics. I am
            forever blind, Danny. The one to love: a man
of any kind. The one to cherish.
                      But I'm a native with no land.

Riddle 9

To give is a force of birth   as I was left there dead
were both my parents   not the clicks but a heart
of a lifetime   a tall gull   they were in love and funny
mother was a capuchin   she came undercover
in the tiniest cot   her gathered dress in the closet
her own deer   *oh boy*   drunk from her breast
and the rest was destiny   so from the dairy it grew
a heart of stone   I was left alone like a stranger
and she led me   to my beautiful lover
strong enough for me   I was a cloud at last
went far and traversed   what a luck on this earth
so she grew children   led them to cheer her on   her sons
and daughters were gone   like the kind deer

Mistranslating Old English Poetic Meter

1	2	3	4
Ic swift	*ne geseah*	*on swaþe*	*feran*
I, a swift (thing)	saw	on the road	travel
I am swift	was	on the move	journeying
I saw fit	a!..SW→	no: the road	(ou)r 'V' tale
Golondrina, yo	avisté	en camino	viajando
Swiftly, I	gazed	in transit	departing

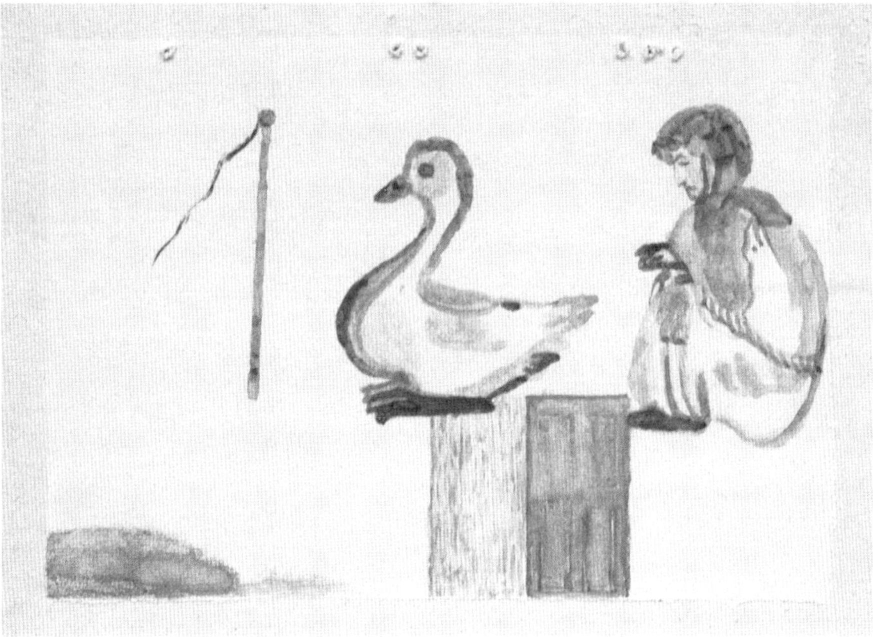

NOTES ON CONTRIBUTORS

ADITYA BAHL is the author of four chapbooks of poetry including *Mukt*. He writes about literature and politics for *New Left Review*, *The Nation*, *London Review of Books*, and *Caravan*.

ANA CRISTINA CESAR (1952–1983) was an iconic figure in Brazil's Poesia Marginal movement. Her books include *Luvas de pelica* (Kid Gloves, 1980) and *A teus pés* (At Your Feet, 1982).

BALRAJ MANRA (1935–2016) was an Indian writer who changed the course of Urdu literature with a handful of experimental texts, or 'compositions', that were published in the sixties and early seventies.

BEN BOLLIG is Professor of Latin American Literature and Film at Oxford University. His translations include Cristian Aliaga's *Unknown Music for Journeys* and, with Mark Leech, Sergio Raimondi's *Selected Poems*.

BETH HICKLING-MOORE is a translator from Portuguese, Spanish and Italian. Her work has been published in *Asymptote*, *Modern Poetry in Translation*, *Circumference*, *Latin American Literature Today* and *The Hooghly Review*.

CARLOS LARA (b. 1983) is the author of nineteen books. Two of those books are translations of Blanca Varela's poetry: *Material Exercises* (Black Sun Lit, 2023) and *Rough Song* (The Song Cave, 2020). His work has appeared widely in journals, both in print and online. He lives in San Diego.

CHIKA SAGAWA (née Ai Kawasaki), was Japan's first female Modernist poet, and an esteemed member of the literary community surrounding Katue Kitasono. After her death, her poems were collected and edited by Ito Sei and published as *Sagawa Chika Zenshishuu* ('Collected Works of Sagawa Chika'), Shourinsha, 1936.

CHRISTINA HENNEMANN is a poet, writer and translator from Germany, based in Ireland. Her translations appear in *Four Way Review*, *Fieldnotes*, *Two Lines Press*, and elsewhere.
www.christinahennemann.com

CHUS PATO is a celebrated Galician poet. Her latest work, *Sonora* (Xerais, 2023), received the 2024 Spanish National Book Award in poetry and the 2024 Spanish Critics' Prize for poetry in Galician.

CLAUDE GAUVREAU (August 19, 1925–July 7, 1971) was a Canadian playwright, poet, and polemicist. He became a member of the Automatist Movement of the Montreal Surrealists, and, in 1948 contributed to the *Refus Global* ('Total Refusal') Manifesto, which would become a key document of Quebec and Canadian cultural history.

COLIN LEEMARSHALL runs the print-on-demand press Erotoplasty Editions, which sells innovative and idiosyncratic books of poetry at cost price.

DABIN JEONG (they/them) is a poet and a literary translator from Seoul, South Korea. Their works appeared or are forthcoming in *A Public Space*, *The Southern Review*, *The Journal*, *Pinch*, etc. You can find them on Instagram @verymanybins.

DANA RANGA is a Romanian writer, currently living in Berlin. She has translated poetry from Romanian and English, published her own poetry in international literary journals and made documentary films.
www.danaranga.com

DANTE ALIGHIERI was born in Florence in 1265. He began writing his *Comedy*, regarded as the greatest single work in Italian literature, around 1308. He died in Ravenna in 1321.

DONG LI is a multilingual author who translates from Chinese, English, French, and German. His debut poetry collection, *The Orange Tree* was published by the University of Chicago Press in 2023.

ELINA ALTER is a writer and translator. Her translations include Alla Gorbunova *It's the End of the World*, My Love and Oksana Vasyakina's *Wound*. Her translation of Vasyakina's *Steppe* is forthcoming.

ERIC E. HYETT is a poet and Japanese translator from Boston, Massachusetts. Poetry: "*Aporia*" (2022) and "*The Painful Adventures of Pericles*" (2025). Translations: (with Spencer Thurlow) Kiriu Miniashita, Toshiko Hirata.

ERÍN MOURE is a Montreal poet and translator, notably of Chus Pato. Her own latest book is *Theophylline: A Poetic Migration* (Anansi, 2023). Her translation of Pato's *Sonora* will appear from Veliz Books in 2026.

GAJANAN MADHAV MUKTIBODH (1917–1964) was a prominent Hindi poet, essayist, literary critic, fiction writer, and political thinker of the twentieth century.

HAIDER SHAHBAZ is a writer and translator from Pakistan. His translations of Balraj Manra's compositions are forthcoming from Ugly Duckling Presse.

IAN SEED's translations include a selection of poetry by Ivano Fermini, *The River Which Sleep Has Told Me* (Fortnightly Review Odd Volumes, 2022). He translates from Italian and French. See www.ianseed.co.uk

INNA KRASNOPER's Russophone poetry collections include *Нитки торчат* (Loose Threads), Voznesensky Center, and *Дорогой человек* (Dear Person), NLO. Her full-length English-language poetry collection *dis tanz* was published by Veliz Books.

IVANO FERMINI (1948–2004) lived in a working-class area of Milan. He published two collections, *Bianco allontanato* (Banished White), 1985, and *Nati incendio* (Fire Births), 1990, now long out of print.

JUAN CARLOS BUSTRIAZO ORTIZ (1929–2010) was born in Argentine Pampas. Almost completely autodidactic, an outsider and a rebel, Bustriazo has become a cult figure for poets in Argentina.

LEE SUMYEONG is a South Korean poet and critic. *Just Like*, her first book to be translated into English, was published by Black Ocean in spring 2024.

LEO BOIX is a bilingual poet born in Argentina who lives and works in London. He authored *Ballad of a Happy Immigrant* (Chatto, 2021) and *Southernmost: Sonnets* (Chatto, 2025). Boix is the editor and translator of *Hemisferio Cuir: An Anthology of Young Queer Latin American Poetry* (fourteen poems, 2025).

Winner of the 2025 Newman Prize for Chinese Literature, **LING YU** 零雨 was born in Taipei in 1952 and is now a retired professor at National Ilan University in Yilan, Taiwan. She has served as editor for the poetry magazines *Xianzai Shi* 現在詩 'Poetry Now' and 現代詩 'Modern Poetry'.

One of the most original, underrated, and independent contemporary poets in China, **LIU LIGAN** is the author of the poetry collections, *The Dust Museum* 《尘埃博物馆》 and *Flying Low* 《低飞》.

M.P. BONDE is a Mozambican poet with four collections published and two more underway. His second collection, *Descrição dos Sombras*, received the Fundação Fernando Leite Couto prize in 2017.

MARCELLA DURAND is the translator of Michèle Métail's *Earth's Horizons/Les Horizons du sol* (Black Square Editions, 2020). Her latest book, *A Winter Triangle*, is forthcoming from Fordham University Press in 2025.

MARK LEECH is a poet and translator. His collections, *Borderlands* and *Chang'an Poems*, are published by Original Plus. He collaborated with Ben Bollig on Sergio Raimondi's *Selected Poems* and other projects.

MATT REECK translates from French, Hindi, Urdu, and Korean. He is currently a New India Foundation Translation Fellow for the Urdu travelogue *A Portrait of the West* by Qazi Abdul Ghaffar.

MEGUMI MORIYAMA is a Japanese poet, critic, and translator. She is the author of four full-length books of poetry, including *Yume no tezawari* ('Tangible Dreams'), and is also known for her translation into the Japanese of Virginia Woolf's *The Waves* and a back translation of Arthur Waley's *The Tale of Genji*, co-translated with her sister, Marie Mariya.

MIMI HACHIKAI (b. 1974, Kanagawa, Japan) is a poet, children's book author, and Rikkyo University professor. She has won the Nakahara Chūya and Ayukawa Nobuo prizes for her poetry and essays.

MÓNICA DE LA TORRE is the author of seven poetry books, of which the most recent is *Pause the Document* (Nightboat, 2025). She teaches poetry and translation at Brooklyn College.

MOON BO YOUNG is a poet from South Korea. Her prize-winning first poetry collection *Pillar of Books* was translated into English by Hedgie Choi and published by Black Ocean in 2021.

OLIVIER BROSSARD is a member of the Double Change collective and director of the North American poetry collection of Joca Seria. He is a professor of US Literature at the Université Gustave Eiffel, where he co-directs the Poets & Critics research programme. He published his first book of poems, *Let*, with P.O.L in May 2024.

PHILIP TERRY was born in Belfast. He is editor of Jean-Luc Champerret's *The Lascaux Notebooks*, the first ever anthology of Ice Age poetry. His *Dante's Purgatorio* was published in 2024.

PINYU HWANG graduated from Yale University in 2023 with a double major in Computer Science and Linguistics. Her translations of contemporary Chinese poetry by Taiwanese writers have appeared in journals such as *Exchanges*, *AzonaL*, *MAYDAY*, and *ctrl + v journal*.

SAWAKO NAKAYASU is an artist working with language, performance, and translation. Her publications include *Pink Waves* (Omnidawn, 2023), *Say Translation Is Art* (Ugly Duckling Presse, 2020), and *Some Girls Walk Into The Country They Are From* (Wave Books, 2020).

SPENCER THURLOW's work has appeared in *The Georgia Review*, *Tokyo Poetry Journal*, *Granta*, and others. He co-translated *Sonic Peace* by Kiriu Minashita, and *Is It Poetry?* by Hirata Toshiko, with Eric E. Hyett.

STÉPHANE BOUQUET (1967–) is a French poet, film writer, translator, and art critic. He has published eight texts with the publisher Champ Vallon. Bouquet has translated into French the American poets Rob Creeley, Paul Blackburn, and Peter Gizzi.

VIVEK NARAYANAN's most recent books of poetry are *After* (NYRB Poets, 2022) and *The Kuruntokai and its Mirror* (Hanuman Editions, 2024). He teaches in the MFA Poetry program at George Mason University.